HUMPED ME, DUMPED ME

About the authors

Yasmin Brooks

Yasmin Brooks works in PR. Based in London, she is currently living it up as an amatory legend. As George Clooney appears to be taken, she is now on a quest to find her very own Mr Right.

Cathy Gray

Cathy Gray is an editor, author and full-time flirt. After years of searching, she has finally found The One and is happily settled in a relationship.

Humped Me, Dumped Me is her third book.

HUMPED ME, DUMPED ME

Why You Were F****d and Chucked and How to Bounce Back

Yasmin Brooks and Cathy Gray

Michael O'Mara Books Limited

First published in 2005 by
Michael O'Mara Books Limited
9 Lion Yard
Tremadoc Road
London SW4 7NQ

A CIP catalogue record for this book is available from the
British Library.

ISBN 1-84317-159-7

1 3 5 7 9 10 8 6 4 2

www.mombooks.com

Designed and typeset by Burville-Riley

Printed and bound in Great Britain by
Cox & Wyman, Reading, Berkshire

Contents

Contents

Acknowledgements

In writing this book we are thankful to many. Although all names in this volume have been changed to protect the identities of the guilty, we must acknowledge these few ex-'gentlemen friends' ... because in all honesty, we couldn't have written a word without them. So, our 'thanks' go to The Architect (the best first date *ever*), The Accountant (hope you passed that audit exam), Groucho Man (words fail us), The 'Sailor' (pink champagne doesn't cover all ills), The Seventeen-Year-Old (appearances can be deceptive), Mr Moët (simply sparkling), The Fitness Trainer ('Sorry' seems to be the hardest word), Mr Nice But No Chemistry (if only), Coffee-Table Man (enough horror stories to rival Stephen King), Mr Nearly Right (so close and yet so far) and, last but not least, Mr Prada Lounge Shoes (keep on running!).

We'd also like to say a huge thank you to everyone at Michael O'Mara Books; to Marc Burville-Riley and Blacksheep Design; to Duncan Moore (for computer facilities ... and so much more); and to our very own GLAMS – ladies, you know who you are!

Yasmin Brooks and Cathy Gray

Introduction:
What a Girl Wants

I t's always the same old story. Boy meets girl. Boy seduces girl. Girl succumbs to his poetic words, pink champagne and passionate declarations – only to wake up in the wet patch, no sign of aforementioned boy and the last bit of Dairy Milk stolen from her secret stash. Millions of women endure this dastardly betrayal weekend after weekend, relationship after relationship. No wonder the dating game is more like dating 'lame' these days.

Well, in the immortal words of Donna Summer, 'Enough is enough'. Forget the ice cream, chocolate and kick-boxing classes: this book will cheer you up, help you out and send you high-fiving your way into the world of men once more, but this time with the insights needed to know the difference between the sure-fire hits and the immature pricks.

Firstly, care not a jot about your marital status. Who really gives a damn? While the single woman has been pigeonholed in the past as a spinster or a dry old maid, and even more modern-day interpretations dismiss her as a SINBAD (Single Income, No Boyfriend, Absolutely Desperate – we have the *Daily Mail* Features Department to thank for that particular reassuring gem), we are of the school of thought that celebrates the single woman as a member of the GLAMS (Gorgeous Ladies After Mini-Break Success). Better still, don't reduce yourself to acronyms. Be an individual, and a fabulous one at that.

Remember, too, that you don't need a man to complete you. You're perfectly whole as you are. However, like bacon and eggs, matching shoes and handbags and Colin Firth swathed in dripping eighteenth-century cotton, the right partnership can complement and enhance your life. Just look at Richard and Judy. This book isn't about hating men or seeing them as sex symbols. It's rather about the fact that finding your perfect partner is a quest on an epic scale (eat your heart out, Frodo), and shows you how to deal with the many monsters you will encounter along the way. Your shining knight may take some time to reach you (public transport isn't what it used to be), so you'd best be prepared for all the finite flings and callous Casanovas that will undoubtedly cross your path in the meantime. But, as this book will reveal, each dalliance is but a building block towards the right relationship – or at least towards a stronger, happier you.

So if a guy dumps you, don't think the world has ended. Topshop is still open! If you get the break-up blues, remind yourself that there are 3 billion men on the planet – so there must be one out there who's right for you. Hold on to the wish list: you want a man who is passionate, funny and respectful, a man who appreciates you and makes you feel you're truly loved. It's the Holy Grail of the modern dating woman (and if he's rich too, you really have struck gold). But if you find yourself with a boyfriend who is none of the above (less Mr Right, more Mr Sub-Standard), it's time to move on. Grab those party shoes, do a quick turn on the dance floor to 'I Will Survive', and then start angling for another fish in the sea.

For *Humped Me, Dumped Me* is certainly not all doom and gloom. It's not only for when relationships go awry and singleton status strikes once more, but it's also your guide to the ultimate flirtatious life, taking in the bars, clubs, chat rooms and speed dates of contemporary courting. Why should men be the only ones to enjoy the bachelor lifestyle? Be a bachelorette: an independent woman having the time of her life.

So why not adopt the following as your mantra? We

have, and believe us when we say we're already reaping the rewards. It's the motto of International Very Good-Looking, Damn Smart Woman's Day (if only there was an official celebration) – and, boy, does it say it all. Live like this and it won't matter whether you're humped, dumped, f****d, chucked, wedded or bedded: you'll be having too much of a good time even to care!

> Life should not be a journey to the grave with the intention of arriving safely in an attractive and well-preserved body, but rather of skidding in sideways, chocolate in one hand, wine in the other, body thoroughly used up, totally worn out and screaming, 'WOO-HOO! What a ride!'

Go for it!

Yasmin Brooks and Cathy Gray
London, 2005

Tragedy

Just when you thought you were practically married with children (or at the very least kept a toothbrush at his flat), the break-up comes from out of the blue. Or, scenario two, you might have been expecting it for weeks. Whatever the circumstances, nothing makes the trauma of a break-up any easier. You can forget about it 'cutting both ways', the pain and punctured pride of a split always feels more like you've just undergone full body surgery – without even the plastic yet perfect figure to show for it afterwards. Despite this, what awaits is still the long and winding road to recovery.

It's a universal and incontrovertible truth that breaking up is hard to do – but it's doubly difficult if you've quite literally been f****d and chucked. Chances are you didn't even get an orgasm out of the experience … so you've been shunned and short-changed: it really is a bloody hard life. Your immediate first thought, naturally, is, Am I really bad in bed? (Trust us, this is unlikely.) The next: Should I have braved that Brazilian? Well, please rest assured on that one too – the male attention span being what it is, he probably wasn't down there long enough to notice your topiary ... if you were lucky enough for him to be down under in the first place, that is. We know men who have split with women because of an infrequency of blow jobs, but God forbid you should ever complain to them about their resounding lack of reciprocation. Frankly, with some men, you're lucky if the foreplay involves anything more than unwrapping the condom (though, clearly, there are others who can take you to seventh heaven with a simple demonstration of their Cadbury's Creme Egg techniques – less 'How do you eat yours?' more 'My God, how do you *do* that?').

As a couple, you may have been together for days, weeks or months (hell, maybe even years – if so, we're impressed), but whatever the length of your liaison, he has now ended it. He's dumped you. Whatever you do, don't auction all your belongings on eBay in recognition of the fact that your life is now officially over – as it most certainly is not. Our view is, don't be a woman scorned, be a woman savvy enough to come out of this with your head held high. Maintain your dignity – at least until he's not around to see you cry. Follow our guide and you'll fool him into thinking that you're totally cool with his decision.

Leaving His Flat Without Losing Your Dignity

Picture the scene. His place. His bed. Post-sex. His pillow talk has just included the immortal phrase 'It's not you, it's me.' Where do you go from here?

1 Reclaim your pants from the lampshade.

2 Go to the bathroom immediately, with a pile of your remaining clothes and an industrial-sized make-up bag.

3 Quickly transform yourself into the goddess that he's about to regret finishing with. (NB: This should take no longer than ten minutes.)

4 Return to the bedroom with Aretha Franklin's 'Respect' running through your head. (Hip-swinging optional.)

5 At this point, try your very hardest to refrain from making any digs about his sexual prowess (namely lack of), size of manhood or personal hygiene. Rise above it (we know, perhaps more

than he could manage five minutes earlier, but this is not the time to mention it). Take the moral high ground and the bitterness won't take you.

6 Gather up belongings, ensuring all jewellery is present and correct. There's nothing worse than making your grand exit, only to have to return two minutes later asking for your watch back. Also account for wallets, mobiles, unusual piercing attachments, stockings and suspenders.

7 This is your cue to leave. You're looking fabulous, you're drawing on reserves of strength and self-respect you never knew you had, and are just moments away from an extra-large Dairy Milk and jumbo Häagen-Dazs. Shrug yourself into your jacket, flick out your gorgeous hair, and pause at the doorway to deliver your parting shot. Any of the following would fit the bill:

a) Well, it's been fun.

b) Don't call me, I'll never call you.

c) Did I mention I won the lottery last week?

or even,

d) I faked it every time...

Well, you're leaving – who cares?

Case Study: Alison

Alison's ex decided to dump her over Christmas (and, as an aside, what is it about men and the Christmas cull – is buying a present really that stressful?). Alison had driven up through snow to see him, and on arrival they settled on the sofa with a bottle of wine. However, it wasn't the cosy scenario you're imagining – instead of festive frolics, this was the moment he chose to break up with her. He delivered the bombshell that he'd only ever slept with her to further his own career (he was a freelancer and she'd commissioned him), and explained that when she came on to him (of course, it was really the other way around) he hadn't wanted to turn her down for fear of losing work. Charming – Merry Christmas everyone. As Alison had been drinking (well, wouldn't you after that kind of shock?), she even had to stay the night after this despicable revelation. We're pleased to report that she remained poised, prim and proud throughout – even though she'd rather have roasted him on an open fire, forget about those chestnuts.

Alison had just the right attitude. When a man has finished with you, it's important to remember to stay cool, calm and collected – even though you're seething inside. We're all for having a good cry, and even the odd dart-throwing session with his photo as the bullseye (actually, that especially), but he'll only feel more sure of his decision if you become hysterical – there's nothing men hate more than an emotional woman, particularly if they're the source of your sadness.

What Not To Do After A Break-Up

....

Don't sleep with him again
Sleeping with the ex is like fancying Richard Madeley: something we all do but don't like to admit to. However, the break-up process inevitably involves one last shag; we advise against it, but in all probability so did your best friend, your hairdresser, the barmaid down the pub, your sister and your friend at work, and let's face it, their advice didn't stop you either. Just go in with your eyes open, enjoy the familiarity, and for God's sake make sure you come this time.

Don't phone or text him late at night or first thing in the morning
He'll only know you're thinking of him and are feeling low. Don't give him the satisfaction. You may well be hibernating in your duvet and wearing your oldest pyjamas, but you

want him to think that you're out partying every night, not giving him a second thought, and you simply don't have the time to get in touch.

Don't slag him off to his mates

Like Carrie in *Sex and the City*, you'll only come out of this looking bitter. And it *will* get back to your ex. Instead, give the friends a fantastic smile and continue having a great night out – even if you're not, slap on a fixed grin and they're sure to report back that you looked flirty and fabulous.

Don't try to make him jealous

Whether it works or not, you're making him the focus – and why should your world revolve around a man? You don't want him back so don't waste your energy. It's your life and he's not welcome in it any more, whether the green-eyed monster makes an appearance or not. Forget about him and move on.

Don't try to analyse why you were dumped

You'll never find out anyway – and sometimes things just don't work out and there is no reason why. Don't dwell on what you might change about yourself – if he doesn't like you for who you are, he doesn't deserve you. This certainly isn't the time for *Extreme Makeover*: trust us, you'll only end up looking ten times worse, and with more scars than an extra in *Casualty*. You're far more fabulous just as you are.

For now, remember the saying that there's always someone worse off than yourself. It's guaranteed to make you feel at least slightly better. Whichever way the ex broke up with you, count yourself lucky if he didn't deliver one of the following 'thoughtful' phrases:

Top Five Worst-Ever Break-Up Lines

5 'I'm really sorry, we can't date any more. That woman you saw me with was my wife.'

4 'I have more fun with my grandmother than I do with you – and she's been dead ten years.'

3 'On a scale of nought to ten, I rate you a six. I'm sorry, but you're just not marriage material – I've really only been killing some time.'

2 'I'm too embarrassed to introduce you to my friends – they don't like fat girls.' (This said to a woman who was a trim size twelve.)

1 'I hate to do this to you and there's really no easy way to say it, but I'm gay.'

When it comes to scheduling the break-up, too, men show about as much tact as Victoria Beckham at a Weight Watchers meeting. Timing is everything, and some blokes choose the worst possible moment to make their move. Let's face it, 'never' would be the only good time for them to break your heart, but if your fella opts for one of the following choice moments, you'll certainly remember him for years to come – and for all the wrong reasons:

Your birthday

Yes, it is your party, and of course you can cry if you want to – but really, who wants to? Destined to make your night fall flatter than a pancake on Shrove Tuesday, getting the push on this particular day always hurts like hell. The only good thing is that all your mates will be there to come to the rescue, and you're bound to be within shouting distance of a double vodka.

At a family gathering

Be it a wedding, funeral, bar mitzvah, christening or just your little sister's eighth birthday party, your man should know that he's only at these events to make you look good. Causing a scene and abandoning you to the mercy of your extended family is not quite the prodigal daughter's triumphant return that you had in mind. And already, the questions from the elderly aunts begin: 'So, when are you going to settle down and find yourself a nice young man?'

The day after his birthday

Oh, he's a wily one. Not to mention materialistic. Having been showered with love, saucy surprises, attention, affection and not a few expensive gifts just the day before, your man now decides that, actually, the relationship isn't going so well. You get the boot, and he gets the birthday booty. *So* not a fair deal. Console yourself with the thought that he is at least another year older now (though, clearly, not much wiser). It can only be a matter of time before the middle-age paunch, receding hairline and grey hairs kick in – and who'll love him then, hmm?

On holiday

The travel brochures were filled with images of loved-up couples meandering along sun-kissed sandy shores; amorous evenings in homely tavernas; and villas featuring passion-prompting four-poster beds. Yet rather than inducing intimacy in your man, the stunning surroundings have instead stimulated his spiteful side. Your anticipation of a restful, romantic break is swiftly crushed – you meander by yourself, use the taverna only as a venue in which to drink yourself into oblivion, and there is no four-poster bed: when the break-up happened, he downgraded you both to separate single rooms. Still, at least that Spanish waiter finds you attractive – and he doesn't just say that to all the girls.

In bed

Common courtesy dictates that he should at least allow you to be fully dressed before he messes with your mind, but some men seem to have forgotten this simple rule of etiquette. Whether the break-up's been brewing in his brain for weeks and simply bursts out without him planning it, or he's just a heartless cad, it's never great to hear you're nothing to him while you're naked. Try to maintain your dignity and get dressed as quickly as possible – or, better still, throw him, still fully starkers, out into the street. Ah, revenge can be so sweet.

))) At the altar

Frankly, an unforgivable offence. Weddings don't just happen overnight. Though the organization is admittedly frantic and tense, he can't have been so busy booking the flowers to have overlooked the fact that he was having doubts. Try to look on the bright side:

1 You look sensational (or, at least, you will imminently, once a speedy retouch of your make-up has removed all traces of distress).

2 You have a new dress.

3 You have a party to attend, at which you will be the indisputed belle of the ball (and that man has paid for at least half of it, so make sure you have a bloody good time).

4 His actions have just saved you from a lifetime of his selfishness, unreliability, stupidity and thoughtlessness. Now, isn't that something worth celebrating?

So, spare a thought for the poor girls who were humped and dumped in this fashion. They took out shares in Cadbury before they bounced back. For you, we hope it will be a much smoother transition from broken-hearted Bridget to bootylicious babe ... albeit with similar strategic cocoa consumption (it's simply *de rigueur* when you've been dumped, after all).

Tears on my Pillow

It's happened: so-called Mr Right has upped and left, without so much as a backward glance. In truth (you may admit to yourself), he was actually more like 'Mr Right Now', but whatever the strength of your feelings for him, the simple fact remains that *no one* likes being dumped. So, how do you recover from your broken heart and/or bruised ego?

One of the following scenarios may apply:

> You are devastated. You really thought
> he was The One.

You were just beginning to get excited about the relationship and out of the blue he's ended it.

In actual fact, it was no great love affair. We are not talking Romeo and Juliet, Scarlett O'Hara and Rhett Butler – or even Sharon and Dennis from *EastEnders* (a love affair of our time, albeit a tragically doomed one). All the same, you liked him and are incandescent with rage that he has had the nerve to dump you – especially if he just pipped you to the post.

Whatever your circumstances, immediately after the dumping has taken place allow yourself some wallow time. Don't feel bad about it; a bit of self-pity never did anyone any harm, and it can be a very cathartic process.

For us, the essential first call after the break-up is to our nearest and dearest girlfriends. They can always be relied upon to rally round with a big box of man-sized tissues (when nursing a broken heart, the standard size just doesn't cut it), and to agree wholeheartedly that you were far too good for him anyway. Obviously, you're much better off without him.

If ever a woman has an excuse to eat ice cream, it's after she's been dumped. See the break-up as a chance for you to sit down and consume a whole tub (in one sitting) without the slightest bit of guilt about the huge calorific implications. These occasions do not come along often – so make sure you savour every single spoonful. (NB: From personal experience, we can highly recommend any of the following ice creams: Organic Green & Black's (any flavour), Häagen-Dazs Belgian Chocolate, Ben & Jerry's Phish Food. Through the years, each has borne the brunt of our most painful break-ups.)

The next – absolutely imperative – move is to delete his numbers from your phone. Don't ever call him, however tempted and/or drunk you may be. The first rule of getting over him is: *Do Not Ever Drink And Dial*. You are upset, so it may seem like a good idea in your fragile emotional state … but it is never a good idea. You have been warned.

You may feel like the world has ended, right now. But it hasn't, honestly. Perhaps annoyingly, the birds still sing, the sun still shines, the soaps still broadcast and the celebrities still go shopping: take a look in *Heat* magazine and you'll see. You may be holed up in your bedroom thinking the end is nigh, but no one else seems to have registered the fact. The world's still out there, and it's waiting for you to rejoin it, whenever you feel ready. Though it will be tough, there is light at the end of the – admittedly very long – tunnel that you're in right now (and we should add, light that signals hope, rather than the headlamps of an express train which is hurtling down said tunnel to put you out of your misery). So remember the following as you're nursing your broken heart, and remind yourself that things will get better, eventually:

Take each day as it comes

It's going to be a while before you feel yourself again, so don't worry about the time it might be taking you to adjust. Rest assured on this: you will be back to normal before you know it. In the meantime, don't panic yourself by thinking about what life now holds (though there are endless, positive answers to that particular question). Instead, just live through each day, moment to moment. Wake up – shower – work – eat – see friends – go to bed. Before you know it, you'll have been single for a week. Then a fortnight. Then a month. And you know, it's not so bad. You survive. You even have fun. And one day, on a day not so very far away from now, you'll wake up … and you'll feel fine.

6 Talk it through

What are friends for, if not to be pseudo-counsellors in your hour of need? Talk through your hurt, anger, pain, humiliation, shock and rage with those closest to you. You never know, they may even have a few pearls of wisdom for you. Were you always so very happy with your man? Your friends may remind you that you moaned about him constantly. Was the sex really that great? They gently prompt that you hadn't had an orgasm for an age. And was he really that handsome? A quick graffiti job on his photo with a black marker, and the truth is there for all to see: no, he was not, and you can do much better for yourself.

Think on the positives

Which may include that famous Tennyson quotation, ''Tis better to have loved and lost / Than never to have loved at all.' The poet knew what he was on about: it's far, far better to have known the joy of love – despite your heartache now – than never to have experienced that amazing roller-coaster ride of romance. And though you're hurting, in time the memories will cease to be painful, and will instead be simply great memories. It may not feel that way at present, but time heals all wounds. After all, your schooldays were a bitch when you lived through them, but there's nothing like dressing up in your old school uniform now, is there? Think on that.

After any relationship split, the weekends can be especially tough to get through – particularly if you're used to waking up together on Saturday and Sunday mornings, snug in your contented coupledom. So here are a few suggestions that might make those down days easier:

If you enjoyed reading the Sunday papers in bed together, why not carry on the tradition? Treat yourself to a glass of Bucks Fizz and a delicious breakfast. Spoil yourself and enjoy the 'me' time as opposed to the 'he' time. Isn't it so much nicer having the newspaper entirely to yourself, and not having to fight him for the colour supplements? Think about the positives, which may include having a whole double bed to yourself – why is it always much more comfortable to sleep diagonally? – and the fragrant scent of a fartless boudoir. Oh, the joy of no more smelly boy!

If you are feeling really down, remember that you don't have to go out and face the world quite yet. If you want to spend the weekend in your pyjamas, do it. This is all part of the process of getting over him. There is no shame in crying into your glass of Chardonnay or Shiraz (depending on your preference) while listening to 'your' song ... that is, if you were lucky enough to have been with him long enough to have had one. (Let's face it, even if it was a one-night stand, the fact that your eyes first met to the strains of 'Hit Me Baby One More Time' will make Britney's entire back catalogue painful listening for ever more.)

Surround yourself with friends. Whether you head over to theirs for a change of scenery and a bit of fresh air, or they come to you to soothe you through your current hell, you'll be amazed at how supportive they can be. If you're up to it, keep yourself busy with social engagements; but if you're not, just sharing a simple supper or a bottle of wine with a friend, or slumping on the sofa together in front of a favourite film, can be all the salvation you need. If you're not quite ready to be on your own in the evenings, make sure you always have someone lined up to help you make it through the night (as Gladys Knight and the Pips once sang so melancholically). Having someone with you keeps the loneliness at bay, especially in the mornings when you wake up and have to remember the break-up all over again. But as we've said, take one day – one weekend – at a time, and the pain will pass.

Weekends are also the perfect opportunity for a few 'life laundry' moments. Store or throw away (whatever is most appropriate for you) any romantic accoutrements that distress you or remind you of him. This can be hugely cathartic. If we're honest, we've all been given gifts that we've pretended to like because our boyfriends bought them for us (chav jewellery and French-maid outfits, anyone?). Now is the time to sell them on eBay, burn them in a funeral pyre or put them in a drawer, never to be seen again. If during this process you start getting angry, remind yourself that you've already wasted far too much time and emotion on this excuse for a man, and that you don't want to waste a moment more. Use the anger to feel empowered. You are a fantastic woman and you don't need his old Valentine cards, emails or iPod playlists of 'your'

songs to remind you of that. Don't get gloomy as you're having your clear-out – think instead of all the space you're freeing up, and all the new things you can fill it with. It's the perfect excuse to go shopping.

So, throw away those man-sized tissues and put the ice cream back in the freezer (if there's any left, that is). Have one last cry (who said panda eyes were unattractive?), listen to 'your' song one last time, and allow yourself one last declaration that you'll never meet anyone like him again (believe us, this is a good thing). It's time to rejoin the world.

Handbags and Gladrags

Right, mourning period over. You can't even remember his name, let alone his favourite colour. The Chardonnay is restricted to girlie nights out on the town, and that chocolate obsession was a whole other you. Now it's time to concentrate on what really matters. No, not whether David Beckham will ever do a nude centrefold (though there's a thought): you now have to concentrate on you.

'Who?' you may say. In all likelihood, you've put other people first for far too long. Your ex, your friends, your family, your colleagues. For the time being, stop worrying about letting people down (you won't be), and instead focus on the one person who really needs your attention. Yes – that would be you again.

First, some pampering. Treat yourself. Meet yourself – underneath all that self-sacrifice is one sexy lady who's probably not been around for a while. It's time to let her take centre stage once more, so strap on some killer heels, slap on some lippy, and venture forth for any of the following 'me, me, me' moments. And don't feel guilty – feel gorgeous.

Haircut and colour

'I'm going to wash that man right out of my hair' is a phrase so accurate it's impossible to believe a man wrote it. Go short, go spiky, go red, go blonde, go black – whatever you fancy will be fabulous. Nothing beats the traditional post-break-up visit to the hairdresser.

Retail therapy

Hit the high street with a vengeance. A new party frock, revolutionary office wardrobe, funky jeans or even a simple sparkly necklace will have you spoiling yourself in the best way known to woman – sartorially. Remember: everything looks great, and nothing is too expensive. It's what credit cards were made for. Besides which, you can never have too many shoes.

Beauty treatments

A soothing massage, refreshing facial, pampering pedicure or mollycoddling manicure is just what the doctor ordered. There's nothing better for making you relax and feel like a million dollars. Don't forget the redeeming benefits of a free makeover at any cosmetics counter either – getting professionally glammed up without a penny spent on products could be, like, *the* best marketing drive ever.

Champagne cocktails

If you can't afford them, there is a usually a well-meaning gentleman near by who can – most importantly, no strings attached. Grab a group of girlies, set yourselves up with a corner table and an ice bucket, and sip from champagne flutes till the caviar comes home. If you can, order everything off the cocktail menu at least once. Well, a girl's got to broaden her horizons, hasn't she?

Girlie nights out with cheesy dancing

(Brie Factor optional depending on your music taste)

Gather a group of friends and prepare for a night out that none of you is going to forget for at least ten years. Spend hours getting ready, complete with compulsory trying on of everything in your wardrobe, dancing round the living room in your underwear to classic hits, and generally getting worked up into a state of excitement a four-year-old high on Sunny Delight would be hard-pressed to beat. Then hit the town, excitably singing Madonna songs at the tops of your voices, to be followed by podium dancing your gran would be proud of, and ending the night by telling your best friend that you 'love her' – no, you really love her. Significantly, drunken lesbian confessions aside, this actually is a night all about friendship, and it's important not to forget it. You, lady, have

come out the other side of being dumped, and your friends are there to celebrate your achievement with you. This is your time for enjoying your freedom on your own terms – it is not a night for pulling (though a little cheeky snog is hardly forbidden fruit), but is rather a statement of independence. For example, you can have seven cheeky snogs if you want to … or, conversely, none at all. The only must is a kebab on the way home – and a declaration in the morning that you will never, ever drink again.

Be fabulous inside and out

Not a call to detox (we think Carol Vorderman does quite enough PR for herself already), but rather a reminder that it isn't all haircuts and gorgeous garments on the road to recovery. You have to look after the inner you too. Sadly, though mates will be there for the dancing and the sobbing, the 3 a.m. phone calls and the rebound catastrophes, you are the only one who can not only mend your broken heart, but fix it in a way that leaves you stronger, happier and more contented with yourself than you ever were before. If this sounds like a tall order, it isn't – it will just take time.

Building up your self-esteem is probably the most important tip we can offer in this book. In short, if you know who you are and what you want, and are strong enough not to compromise or 'settle' for a sub-standard relationship, you have the  best possible chance of finding a partner who will fulfil you in every way imaginable. In our opinion, that's worth holding out for.

There is no magic recipe for being happy with yourself, and self-confidence is certainly not something discovered overnight – especially if you've just had it knocked for six by some unmentionable man. Remember the following key points, though, and you've a great start to build on...

1 You're better off without him

A cliché, we know, but no less true because of that. Remember that the relationship wasn't working – if not for you, then certainly not for him, and who wants to be with a man not fully appreciative of all your amazing qualities?

2 It's better to be single and happy than in a relationship and miserable

Frankly, a motto that every girl should adopt. We're all for trying to sort things out if there's a relationship worth saving, but there's simply no point in trying to do the heroic thing by going down with the ship ... especially when there are plenty more fish in the sea. (Enough marine mixed metaphors, do you think? Apparently nautical is making a comeback this season.) If he makes you unhappy, get out. See point one – you're better off without him.

3 Being in a relationship doesn't define you

Have the strength to stand on your own two feet. Even when you're in a couple, the pair of you are still two individuals. Don't forget that who you are has nothing to do with your marital status – you're the same great, occasionally moody, often flamboyant, regularly brilliant person with or without a man. In our opinion, too, you're more likely to find Mr Right if you know yourself and therefore what you're looking for. He's less likely to dominate you with his personality – and vice versa. So be as brave or as bolshy or as timid as you like: you don't have to please anyone but yourself with your personality, and your personality is something unique to you. Be proud of it.

4 Have inner worth

There's only one thing to say about self-respect: never forget to have it, own it, work it, love it. This is the best possible tip for avoiding unhappiness and for having a life you love. Never settle: you are worth more. Be happy. Be fun. Be fabulous. Be the best flirt this country has ever seen.

Feeling fired up yet? Then it's time to get back out there. World: get ready. Lady: get set. Three, two, one … we have lift-off!

It's Raining Men

When it comes to meeting a man – specifically, one who makes you sit up and take notice, as opposed to just any old Joe – the key thing to remember is that it could happen at any time. In all honesty, it's most likely to happen when you're really hungover, wearing your oldest, most unflattering outfit and haven't washed your hair for days. That's when Mr Rights have a habit of suddenly shopping in your local supermarket, or appearing poised like superheroes on the stairs of your apartment building (a miracle that has never once happened before in the entire three years you've lived there). But worry not about those lanky locks – if opportunity and Mr Right are ripe, just go ahead and bite, bite, bite.

It may happen when you least expect it: on the journey home after a rubbish day at work; while you're waiting for a friend (who has just phoned to say she'll be half an hour late, giving you ample time for a quick coffee with a passing Casanova); on the other side of the world, halfway through a globetrotting trip. All too often, however, these unexpected meetings can be far too infrequent – or, conversely, throw up all manner of weirdos, inappropriates and undesirables, so that after your sixth hellish dating experience with Mr Unexpectedly Met, you're crying out for a nice boy who just knows how to wash and can string a sentence together using words of more than one syllable.

Step forward the world of the modern date. In our increasingly segregated society – where it's impossible to meet your neighbours, let alone your match – finding a decent man has become an industry. Seriously. Type 'dating' into an Internet search engine and good old Google will return over 49 million hits. And that's just the World Wide Web; the clubs, pubs, bars, gyms, phone lines and friends of friends don't even get a look-in here. There are literally hundreds of ways to meet men, and each provides its own cache of different types: your online dating service, for example, will turn up someone quite distinct from the frequenters of the Aussie-favourite Walkabout pubs. So, you must select your source of sauce with care. We truly believe that there is someone out there uniquely tailored to each and every one of us; similarly, there will be a way of finding him that will perhaps suit only you. Not for everyone the speed date or the blind encounter; not for everyone the chat room or the club.

Listed below are just some of the methods and venues available to the modern woman in her amatory quest – you may scoff at some, but others will ring-ding-ding your bell with glee, and it's best foot forward and into the fray.

Be warned: at times the dating world is a bitch. You will meet so many Mr Wrongs that it can be demoralizing. We admit that. We know that. The important thing to remember is that this love lark is supposed to be fun. So what if you're on the worst date ever? Laugh about it with your mates afterwards. So what if he and you are so unsuited you've spent the entire evening chatting about the weather? It's all grist to the mill. Oscar Wilde once wrote that 'Experience is the name everyone gives to their mistakes' – that is certainly so, but making those mistakes can be marvellous. Just move on from them and go with the flow. You may even learn something from these disastrous dates – for example, an unwanted approach in a bar once led to us being given the most informative analysis of financial investment we've ever had. And that's not a euphemism.

One other word of advice – if Method X hasn't worked for you so far, don't be afraid to try Method Y. We know, you never thought that a pretty, personable, sophisticated and mature young woman such as yourself would be sitting opposite twenty guys in one evening with just three minutes with each to make your mark ... but go with it. You never know when you might strike gold. You never know if it's this night or  the next. You can only put yourself out there – try new things, meet new people, be happy and flirty and fun. And, one day or another, you never know ... you just might meet The One.

⑥ Friends of friends

A most excellent way of meeting people. Generally, you can be sure he's not an axe murderer – a very good start indeed. Someone you know, and hopefully like, knows and hopefully likes him too. So there's a shared friendship connection – and a chance that that kindred chemistry might bubble over into 'something more'. In addition, the 'friends-of-friends' encounters usually happen organically. There may be the odd blind date where your friend gets to do her Cilla Black bit (though hopefully without the make-up and the wig), but more frequently there will be a barbecue, a party, a night out down the pub, where the two of you can meet and chat and ... bingo! A date in a couple of nights' time.

Buses and trains

Often an untapped resource. Jennifer, travelling home alone one night after an evening out with friends, made eye contact with a man and there was an instant connection. They exchanged a few flirty looks, and laughed when they both disembarked at the same bus stop. Jennifer, in high spirits and not backward in coming forward, started chatting to him. Luckily, he was unattached and more than interested. Cue in-the-street snogging (somewhat less than classy – but somehow oh so passionate), a request to take her out to dinner the following night and an exchange of business cards and contact details. He turned out to be not quite so fabulous the following evening, but a free meal and the opportunity to practise her flirtation techniques meant that the encounter was far from wasted.

Similarly, there's Rachel's tale: a crammed train carriage after the rugby. A rumble in her tummy – it's been hours since lunch and she has a craving for sweetness like you wouldn't believe. Suddenly, she sniffs the air. Among the BO of the armpits thrust in her face is another much more heavenly scent:

chocolate. Across the carriage, she spies the object of her lust: a Yorkie bar. She stares, she salivates, and she notices what (or rather who) is attached to the treat: a six-foot, gorgeous, eligible hunk. She stares, she salivates. He catches her eye: he's been watching her watching the chocolate. He offers; she accepts. They get chatting, they get flirting, the situation sizzles. All too soon, the train pulls into her station (so to speak). An exchange of numbers, a few meaningful looks, and she exits with both chocolate and a potential date. A job exceedingly well done.

'Extracurricular activities'

... As they used to be called at school. By this we mean the gym, the drama group, charity volunteer work, rowing club, etc., an activity probably separate from your usual social circle, which automatically widens it, as well as broadening your ability to converse on a range of topics (a skill always useful when on a nightmare date). Appropriately enough, involvement with a group you may be passionate about frequently leads to passions of an entirely different kind ... and we're not talking ground-breaking Mel Gibson movies here. Sarah joined her amateur-dramatics group because she missed performing. Over the course of rehearsing a play, she not only made dozens of new friends but fell madly in love with her director (she attributes it to his amazing theatrical vision – we're more suspicious of a Kate Winslet/Sam Mendes obsession ourselves). Whatever your 'extracurricular activity' – and snogging behind the bike-sheds doesn't count – chances are that meeting people with similar interests may well lead to a meeting of minds and, ahem, even bodies. Most importantly, make sure that if you take up a new hobby it is something you actually fancy doing with your spare time: abseiling down the sides of mountains is all very well and may indeed introduce you to chiselled, sporty types, but isn't so good if you get vertigo and are vomiting in their faces every ten metres.

☃ Speed dating

The route to relationships for twenty-first-century singletons. The key to having a good speed-dating experience is to choose your venue with care. Go to a bar you'd happily spend a normal night out in, a place

where the clientele seem like 'your kind of people'.
Check the age range of your night too: pity Sam and
Amelia, ladies in their early twenties who found
themselves faced with men nearly twice their age,
who were so overcome at the sight of the 'youngsters'
that it was less 'sugar daddy' and more 'chocolate
fondue fountain with extra marshmallows and
chocolate drops ... and I apologize for dribbling all
over you (I forgot to put my teeth in).' Not a happy
experience. When speed dating, be yourself, be
honest about who you'd like to see again, and enjoy
any dates that come your way. They won't all work
out, but isn't it lovely to be wined and dined
anyway?

⛵ Globetrotting and the holiday romance

Sometimes, you have to go halfway round the
world to meet The One. Amanda was staying in a
youth hostel in Sydney when she met her man: a
lone traveller just returned from the outback who
had more facial hair than a Yeti. Freshly shaved,
he turned out to be foxiness personified: they
ended up living together in Oz, and six months
later, on their return to Europe, she moved from

Northern Ireland to 'mainland' Britain to be with her bloke. Four years on, they're inseparable, and the wedding's just a matter of time (apparently, the proposal will come once she stops talking about it ... typical man!). Travelling can be an eye-opening, mind-blowing, self-finding opportunity – add 'soulmate-sourcing' to the list and you're right on. Look around your temporary community of backpackers and fellow beach babes – is there anyone who might be just that little more permanent?

₥ Internet dating

Be it 'official' dating sites, romantic weblinks or charming chat rooms, the Internet offers a whole host of possibilities for pulling. You may meet someone like-minded on a fansite or in a debate forum – alternatively, you could do worse than sign

up to the sites which offer pictures, mini-biographies and practically a review rating on each potential date, not to mention the chance of emailing him prior to meeting up. Natasha had a string of dates from her online dating service before meeting Neil. Something clicked with them (and we don't mean their mice), their dates became a relationship, that relationship led to their moving in together, and two years on they're now trying for a baby. They're also proud of how they met: the image of the Internet being 'just for nerds' is completely old hat these days, and sexy, professional, socially competent people all use it for its dating potential. As with any blind date – however well you think you know him beforehand – always make sure someone knows where you're going, not only for the safety aspect but also so that all your friends know you have a hot date. Discussing it beforehand is half the fun, isn't it? (Occasionally, we admit, *all* the fun, but let's not dwell.)

Bars and clubs

Perhaps the most regular way of meeting the opposite sex. And, agreed, often, with this method of meeting a man, 'meeting' on these occasions may well actually translate to 'exchanging saliva and tongue-rotating techniques before having a good old fumble' ... particularly if that tequila bottle has done the rounds an hour or so earlier. We would say two things regarding your bar and club conquests:

1   Just because you've already kissed/heavy petted/slept with him, it doesn't mean that this can't be the start of something slightly more serious and long term. We none of us are Cinderella these days: she only 'put out' a glass slipper before a proposal of marriage came winging her way. Lucky cow. (Mind you, she married into the royal family, and we all know how that can turn out.) If you like him, pursue it – get his number, suggest meeting up again ... even if it transpires to be simply for Round Two.

2   On the other hand, meeting a man in a bar doesn't mean you have to 'get down' with him right there and then – even if Christina Aguilera's 'Dirrty' is playing and you're as horny as Rudolph on 24 December (though hopefully without the alcohol-induced red nose). Use your budding chemistry as the basis for a later dinner date, or a one-on-one meeting where you can really get to know one

another (and not necessarily in the biblical sense of the word).

Take Adam and Claire, who met on the dance floor of a Hawaiian-beach-themed bar. Leaving aside that dubious venue, Claire liked Adam's moves and when he left the dance floor and stepped out to the patio, she took it as a sign to follow. (He later admitted that he was actually going for some air – one too many pints and all that – but Claire apparently failed to notice his deep breaths and rather green face, or put it down to nerves.) They kissed that night and excitably exchanged numbers; six months later, they were engaged. Surprisingly, given the bar they met in, we've been assured that 'I've Got A Lovely Pair Of Coconuts' is unlikely to accompany their first dance. Such a disappointment.

In summary, then, meeting Mr Right could happen any time, any place: he could be anyone. So never be too hasty in brushing men off. It's rare to find love at first sight (lust is, of course, a different matter), and don't fail to account for your own short-sightedness – like Bridget and Mark Darcy, Harry and Sally, and Joey and Pacey, very often it's the men right under our noses who turn out to be the men we want to know more about. Be receptive and friendly and flirty and fun – and who knows what could follow? The office, the station, the stage or the beach: the world is your oyster. Now here's hoping for some pearls.

Holding Out For A Hero

I n truth, none of us are virgins in the dating game. You will already have utilized any or many of the methods we've mentioned in your quest to find Mr Right. But this time something's different. Armed with the following information, you'll be nobody's fool. No more the victim of the on-the-make man, instead you'll be the one in charge and in control. This is how to spot the men to steer clear of ... those men who are just not worth bothering with.

The player

. . . .

You can spot this one a mile off – and don't even kid yourself that you can be the one to make him change his ways. Key things to look out for are the big ego and the arrogant attitude, the wardrobe full of designer suits, and the 'shag pad' (their own flat, where the bedroom is suspiciously neat and tidy because they knew they'd pull someone that night, they always do). These men are completely committed to serial shagging – they are not looking for a relationship, they are only looking for sex. For them, three dates would constitute marriage. Also look out for mirrored ceilings, silk sheets, and champagne chilling in the fridge.

Case Study: Stelios

A gentleman who can only be described as a man about town. He has looks, charm and conceit – and the chat-up lines to match. Out one night, he spies a likely young lady and makes a beeline for her (tonight's her lucky night). He starts his spiel. However, he fails to notice her equally lovely friend, a lady who had been the object of his attention just the week before. Said friend cuts into his seduction:

'You don't recognize me, do you? Last week you were saying exactly the same things to me. But don't mind me – carry on talking to her.' Not surprisingly, our Lothario is suddenly rendered speechless and slinks away a few moments later – taking the attitude that lightning never strikes in the same place twice, even with his skills.

The player is also only interested in himself. Forget shared conversation about mutual interests, and don't even hope that he'll ever ask anything about you. This is a man who thinks that Galileo had it all wrong: clearly, the world revolves around him. Take David, an actor who thought the way to get women into bed was through reeling off his (less than) impressive CV, together with casual nonchalance about cocaine-fuelled parties and networking in Cannes. Already a big turn-off. As if these self-centred stories weren't bad enough, David's flat held yet more horrors. In the living room sat a coffee table like no other coffee table seen before. Two huge lion cubs, made of technicolour porcelain, gambolled beneath a large glass table-top. In his words, this monstrosity added a 'touch of

Africa' to the room. However, it was more tacky *Footballers' Wives* than Tanzania. Our player *didn't* pull that night.

As an aside, a man's home reveals a lot about him. Dreadful décor may well translate into a disastrous date – especially if he's cooking for you at home. 'Interesting' pieces, wacky wall-coverings and mould-covered cutlery do not a happy woman make. Diane once had a date with a very sexy Australian man. The chemistry between them was intense and her thoughts throughout the evening were less *Home and Away*, more home, home, home! Finally, hands all over each other, they arrived back at his place. Talk about a cold shower ... not that you would even have dared enter the bathroom. His flat was disgusting – dirty, messy, and with seventies-inspired wallpaper that would have cooled even John Travolta's fever. Needless to say, Diane hotfooted it home – she wasn't getting naked in that environment, even though her date had a body to die for. Given what might have been growing in those sheets, 'to die for' may well have been the operative term.

The mummy's boy

• •

Essentially, he sees you as good enough to shag, not good enough to marry. These men respect their mothers' opinions so much you will never live up to their expectations. You will always be too short, too fat, too common or just too average to make 'wife material'. The mummy's boy can be difficult to identify, as he will always be polite, thoughtful and up for monogamous commitment – but only ever in the short term. Watch out for frequent mentions of the family and especially very regular visits home. If she's still doing his laundry, it's definitely no go. Sally knew early on that her man was a mummy's boy – on their first (and only) dinner date, he spent forty minutes on the phone to his mother, leaving her sitting alone staring into her starter. We can tell you now that bruschetta grows boring after three minutes, let alone another thirty-seven. She was just pleased she hadn't ordered soup.

Case Study: Ben

Ben having seduced Maria, they ended up back at his place the morning after the night before. Ben, keeping it in the family, lived with his sister, and insisted upon Maria meeting her. Our heroine protested vehemently but to no avail. Let's face it, you never want to meet your boyfriend's sister when you're wearing last night's clothes. Immediately, Maria was on the back foot, and as we all know that's not a good foot to be on. It didn't take a genius to work out that his sister was not impressed (maybe it had something to do with the disdainful looks across the breakfast table), and Maria suddenly found herself relegated to the type of girlfriend who was only ever going to be a short-term prospect.

The oddball

These are the men with no social skills. The strange ones. More at home at a *Star Trek* convention than in a bar. They are usually met when their good-looking mate is chatting up your friend. Obviously you have to be polite (especially if your friend is rather taken with his), but don't be too encouraging. The problem with oddballs is that they're pretty hard to shake off once they're smitten. Head them off early with fabricated tales of a boyfriend out of town before you have to endure the embarrassment of them trying to impress you.

Case Study: Robert

A sad, lonely figure who could down a pint in three gulps if he realized no one was talking to him and it was time to go home. If he found a willing ear for conversation, his chat would consist of the witty statement 'Well, isn't this interesting?' to describe being in a bar on a Friday night. Jessica worked with him and found herself agreeing to a few drinks one-on-one post-5.30. That night turned into a few occasional dinners, but the evenings were more like therapy sessions than dates: she just felt sorry for him and was trying to boost his self-esteem. Sadly, he took it a bit more seriously than that and she was forced to make the break.

Mr Lame

The men who just can't get their act together, even if they are actually interested in you. Arranging a date can take weeks or even months. You never know where you stand – all your communication with him is fantastic; he makes you laugh, the chemistry sizzles, when you see each other it's great … but when it comes to fixing up dates or simply making a move he's soggier than a wet weekend in Bognor. These men have never heard the phrase 'Seize the day' – and you'll be lucky if they ever even attempt to seize you (the term 'damp squib' springs to mind). All evidence suggests that he's keen on you, but his interest comes in fits and starts; these guys are like temperamental cars on a frosty morning – the engine keeps cutting out, you're repeatedly trying the starter (to no avail), and even when that works it takes an age to get things moving.

Case Study: Tom

Tom met Lydia at a party where they got on fabulously, but (of course) he didn't ask for her number. She was a little disappointed but thought nothing of it, just put it down as one of those flirtations not destined to go anywhere (how right she was, in retrospect). A month after the bash, Lydia received an email from Tom – he'd made the effort to track her down via a mutual friend. All well and good, though she felt that this endeavour was a bit of an afterthought; why didn't he ask for her details the night they met? Regardless, she replied. His email hadn't asked for a date, so their initial contact was purely pleasantries. Conversations followed, Lydia confused by his flurry of text messages and random phone calls, which never once mooted the idea of meeting up. She couldn't work him out – did he want to be friends; if so, why was he sometimes flirtatious?

Eventually, three months after they first met, Tom suggested a rendezvous. Lydia was stunned – their contact was so fleeting that she had in all honesty forgotten about him. She wasn't sure she'd even recognize him if she passed him in the street. However, his email was contrite, apologetic and enthusiastic, so she decided to give him the benefit of the doubt (more fool her). On the date, Tom was half an hour late, talked only about himself, left after one drink to meet up with his work colleagues, and topped it all off with an email the following week (time moves slowly in Mr Lame's world) explaining that he was very busy so couldn't see her again for a while, but it had been 'good to chat'. Lydia couldn't believe it – after the way he'd behaved, he thought she was still interested? She had obviously already written him off – if the first date had taken three months to organize, she'd be past childbearing age by the time he got around to the first kiss.

The man who belongs to someone else

These men are notoriously difficult to spot. The gentlemen in question are Oscar-winning liars who will helpfully never tell you themselves that they're attached, and think nothing of removing wedding rings, photos from wallets and their pants in their quest to get you into bed. If you're not entering into the affair knowingly, you'll probably only discover the existence of his other half after you've completely fallen for him. However, here are some warning signs to watch out for, which may well rumble them before you get your heart broken:

☆ Regularly cancelling dates at the last minute, usually without a good reason.

☆ Texting rather than calling you. (Although, having said that, remember that men are famously bad at communication and you may simply have landed a bloke who doesn't like to chat.)

☆ Late-night communication or only hearing from him during the day – never ever in the early evening when he's probably just delivering his 'Hi honey, I'm home!' line.

☆ Not being available to meet up over the weekends.

☆ Refusing to let you meet his friends – something always comes up.

☆ Showing a keen willingness to stay at your place rather than his, and refusing to show you his home.

☆ When he does stay over at yours, regularly leaving very early in the morning, and often not staying the whole night. If this is the case, he really is attached. He's leaving because he belongs with someone else.

Case Study 1: John

Nicola first met John at the gym. As happens, they grew close over time and began dating. Everything seemed wonderful but the reality was quite different. He was promising holidays (that never worked out), exciting dates (for which he was either late or a no-show), and even talked of their moving in together. But before that could happen, there was the small issue of his wedding – and he wasn't marrying Nicola. Now she knew the reason why, after a year of being together, she'd never seen his flat – and it wasn't because of his so-called 'sick' father, whom he'd said had been staying with him. In fact, Nicola found out about the ceremony two weeks after it had taken place and, crazily, worked out that she'd seen John the morning of his wedding. Talk about duplicity. Nicola's year-long investment in her 'relationship' turned out to be totally worthless: the relationship was founded entirely on lies. John even wanted to keep seeing her after she found out the truth – it simply beggars belief.

Case Study 2 (and believe us, there are plenty more): Harry

Harry cracked on to Lisa one night as Valentine's Day approached. Clearly a romantic at heart, he wanted to pin her down for a date on the special day itself. She was thrilled – until he laid his ground rules. He'd have to be off by ten, he explained, as he needed to meet his girlfriend then (she'd be busy earlier in the night, as she had a date with her husband. We promise this is indeed a true story!). Lisa, not willing to be the bit on the side's bit on the side, spent Valentine's night with her girlfriends. Clever lass.

So there you go. Watch out for the players, the mummy's boys, the oddballs, Mr Lame and those men who belong to someone else, and you have a much better chance of identifying someone who may well be Mr Right.

Murder on the Dance Floor

I t's now time to put your new-found knowledge into practice. Across the world, for the single woman, Friday and Saturday nights have assumed a significance to rival the opening of the Harrods sale. Week after week, the weekend ritual of cocktails and clubbing (undertaken in the hope of finding a cute man) is approached with the utmost seriousness. Fuelled by memories of Patrick Swayze and Jennifer Grey in the seminal *Dirty Dancing*, every woman hopes to meet her match on the dance floor. Sadly, the footwork displayed by most men these days leaves a little to be desired (think Ricky Gervais in *The Office* as opposed to Ricky Martin), but nonetheless the nightclub continues to be the most successful hot spot when seeking a man.

First step: pull on your disco-diva dress and your party shoes. Every girl has a sure-fire pulling outfit secreted in her wardrobe – that black corset or that fabulous denim mini – so if you're on a mission there's absolutely no clothing choice to make: you know exactly what to wear to make it a night to remember. Put that outfit on and someone else is guaranteed to take it off ... that is, if you want them to.

So after a few drinks in a bar, the nightclub calls. Your success rate here will depend upon what vibes you're giving off that night. Are you:

a) In a foul mood?

If you'd rather be slumped on the sofa with a packet of Pringles watching re-runs of *Friends*, tonight is just not going to be your night. To be honest, you should quit now: you're so ready to be disappointed that no man will meet your high standards, and if you do happen to spot someone who takes your fancy, they'll take one look at your sour face and head for the hills.

b) On a mission?

Forget the Secret Service, James Bond has nothing on you: you're ready to be shaken and stirred. From the moment you step into the club and target your object of desire, nothing is going to come between you and your man. You make a beeline for him and work it till he's putty in your hands, casting your net until he's fallen for you hook, line and sinker. Mission accomplished.

c) Desperate?

Never a good vibe. If your chat-up line consists of 'I'm going to be thirty in two months and I want to be married and pregnant by my birthday,' it's safe to say you'll be celebrating the big day on your own. Though everyone is surreptitiously on the lookout for that someone special, casing the joint with the dedication of a professional burglar is just not cool.

d) Feeling flirtatious?

When all you're looking for is a fun night out. If that involves boogying on the bar with seven male 'backing dancers' to enhance the routine, then so be it – but finding a man is not the be-all and end-all tonight (though a cheeky snog would be nice). Instead, you're simply strutting your stuff on the dance floor (Kylie, eat your heart out) and men are dropping at your feet like flies.

How To Tell If You're A Turn-On

Six chat-up lines that let you know when you're scorching hot to the opposite sex:

'My God, you've got a great body. I could snort cocaine off your hipbones.'

'I know it's a cliché, but I could swim in your eyes for ever. Would you save me if I drowned?'

'You've got the body of a racehorse and I want to ride all night.'

'I think you're really toxic.' (Spoken to the strains of Britney's classic hit – please, show some originality.)

'I couldn't help noticing that you have a stunning figure. I'm a personal trainer – I'd love to put you through your paces.' (This from a very smooth New Yorker – press-ups not normally leading to passion, our leading lady didn't ever call.)

'Your skin is so amazingly soft. You've got the softest skin I've ever known.' (Your response, 'Well, I do moisturize.')

But whatever vibes you're giving off, remember that there's always a lot of competition. It's a jungle out there and, as in the animal kingdom, there are predators at every turn: it's a case of survival of the fittest. If you've spotted a foxy male, the chances are that several other single women have too. Although strictly speaking the rule is 'every woman for herself', it's a different matter entirely if the competition comes from one of your own friends. In our opinion, there's a certain etiquette that should be followed – and stealing a friend's pull really isn't in the spirit of sisterhood. In short, if a lady has identified a real humdinger, it's definitely a case of 'hands off' for her homies.

Case Study: Anna

A six-foot maiden in need of a tall Prince Charming, she always counted herself lucky if there was more than one man on the dance floor above her eyeline (this even before taking into consideration whether he was attractive or not). Nightclubs for Anna were like walking into a Short Man Convention. Imagine her joy, therefore, when she spied a man one night who was six foot five and to die for. Immediately, she went to make her move. Things started off well – conversation was flowing, drinks had been bought and there was more than a bit of flirtation from both sides. Unfortunately for Anna, however, her group of 'friends' included Holly. Now this young lady wasn't exactly renowned for choosing her mates over her men. In fact, if you had just been rescued from a burning building (well, it might just happen), Holly would be chatting up the firemen rather than checking on your welfare. Friendship wasn't high on her list of priorities. On the night in question, despite Holly being a mere five foot three, she too decided that Mr Gorgeous was the man for her – and steam-rollered in to make him her own. Ignoring Anna's fantastic progress with her pull, Holly physically took hold of the man, moved him towards her, and they locked lips with a speed that would stun even Jodie Marsh. Anna, meanwhile, was left open-mouthed – and with not a tongue in sight.

Provided you have triumphed over everyone else in securing your pull's attention (and vice versa, of course; sometimes you're the one with the multiple choices), the next move is always the first drink. Generally, it's a good idea to accept his offer – but make sure you're at the bar to see the drink being mixed, as you can't be too careful these days. Having drinks with a man is a chance for both of you to test the water – will your conversation sink or swim? If it's the former, finish your drink and politely excuse yourself – you need the loo or to find your friends ... or simply assume your 'help me' face, which summons a rescue party (i.e. your mates, rather than Michael Buerk with the camera crew from *999*) to whisk you off to the dance floor to meet some further contenders. Certainly don't feel you owe him anything just because he bought you a vodka and cranberry – or even because he fought for your country. Emma was faced with this line when she was chatted up by an army officer who had just returned from Iraq. He seemed to think that his military efforts entitled him to his pick of the ladies. When she turned him down, he turned nasty, citing his bravery and heroics in an attempt to get her into his arms. She wasn't impressed and gave him his marching orders – and thought it best not to mention she was actually anti-war.

The dance floor can be the best place for meeting men. After all, men can get tongue-tied, but here there's no need for scintillating conversation or cheesy chat-up lines – he can simply move next to you, look wishful, shake his stuff and hope to catch your eye. But there comes a time when he has to speak, so here are a few classic opening gambits:

🦋 'I say, you're a great dancer! Do carry on.'

🦋 'How tall are you?' (Answer: five foot eleven-and-a-half – well, he did ask.)

🦋 He sings: 'Man, I feel like a woman!' (Perhaps not quite what Shania had in mind.)

🦋 'I've never seen anyone dance the way you do without paying money for it first.'

🦋 As he tries to impress you with his slick moves – 'I was in *Riverdance*, you know.'

🦋 'So, what do you do then?' (Talk about a turn-off – discussing your career on the dance floor is a definite no-no.)

On occasion, neither drinks nor dancing are needed to get the party started. Sometimes there is instant chemistry the moment you lock eyes with a man – if it's not love at first sight, it's most certainly lust (that denim mini is *so* working its magic). Charlotte once scored within sixty seconds of entering a club, a better record than any recent England striker (though clearly scoring skilfulness is a different matter for the management). Charlotte made eye contact, he made the move, and they were snogging before you could say 'Success!' Happily, Charlotte's triumph didn't entail cutting the night short for her friend, instead the quick-fire conquest proved inspirational, and it was game, set and match for both ladies that night. Sometimes you and your friends will all be in the same mindset and will hit the jackpot simultaneously, making you all winners. It's like the domino effect – one falls and you all follow.

So, however you and your man's paths crossed, you are now motoring on the road to romance. You've moved, you've grooved – it's now up to you whether you want to bump and grind. If his kissing technique is sloppier than a St Bernard's, there'll be no more heavy petting for that particular puppy. If on the 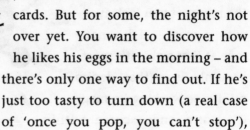 other hand you want to see him again, you might have exchanged numbers, in which case a date could be on the cards. But for some, the night's not over yet. You want to discover how he likes his eggs in the morning – and there's only one way to find out. If he's just too tasty to turn down (a real case of 'once you pop, you can't stop'), chances are you won't be heading home alone. It's going to be one of those nights...

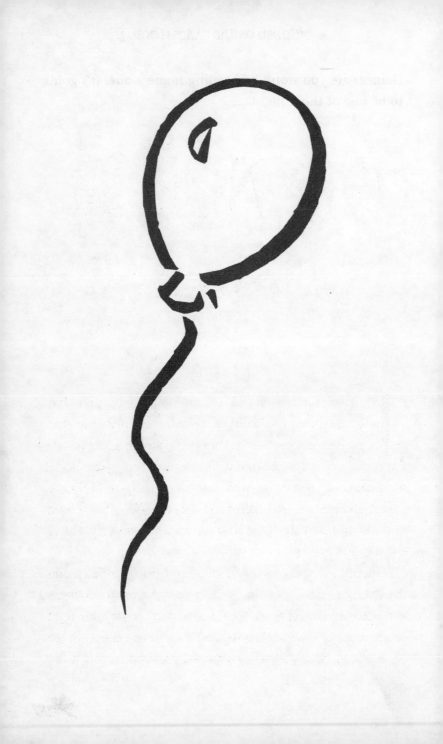

One Night in Heaven?

The one-night stand, for better or worse, has established for itself a permanent place in the modern dating world. Whether indulging in one last fling with the ex, sampling the delights of your local nightclub, or getting intimate with an impossibly tasty friend, chances are that each and every one of us has at least one notch on our bedpost that represents a single night of passion and not(ch) much more.

Naturally, despite the one-night stand being prevalent on the dating scene, it remains a liaison fraught with problems and potential danger areas. Your place or his? To stay the night or not to stay the night? Hamlet had it so much easier with 'To be or not to be' – that was existential philosophy, this is the minefield of mingers, masochists and the morning after the night before. A one-night stand is rarely planned but if you do end up sleeping with a stranger, remember the following:

ᕙ DO use protection

This should go without saying. Be safe. If he won't use protection then head for the door immediately. We all know the dangers of putting safety second – STDs are rife and don't discriminate. They can happen to you so don't under any circumstances put yourself at risk.

⟲ DO make sure you know what you want from your one-night stand

If you're looking for long-term love and commitment, it's perhaps best to walk away right now. No doubt some meaningful relationships do blossom from these fleeting flings, but whether they're still flowering six months down the line is a rather more dubious prospect. If you're looking for a night of passion with no strings attached, however, or for some brief intimacy (it gets lonely sleeping on your own), you've come to the right place. Decide ahead of time how you want to play it: are you simply looking for a night of excitement, or do you really like this man and hope to see him again? Are you going to get emotionally involved? It will save you a lot of heartache and bother if you sort out your state of mind right from the very start.

Case Study: Emily

As soon as she brought Damon home and saw him in some decent lighting (a darkened nightclub may well be atmospheric, but can be thoroughly misleading), she knew their fling would be short-lived. Rather like a vampire, it wasn't set to survive the sunrise. Damon was clearly a lot younger than he'd originally said, and Emily had already endured the trauma of A levels once – she wasn't going to suffer it again vicariously. Her mind was made up when she asked what he might be doing later in the day – 'Helping Mum with some chores' wasn't quite the answer she was expecting. Damon asked to see her again, but Emily sent him packing in the early hours. It was just as well – he probably had a paper round to get up for in the morning.

6 DON'T get in too deep emotionally

After all, whatever physical intimacy is involved, you've only just met this guy. How can you possibly know if you're compatible beyond the bedroom? Be vigilant about not letting the transient closeness cloud your vision. He may be holding you in his arms right now, but that's no guarantee you'll hold on to him tomorrow. Take what you need from the conquest – perhaps a boost to your self-esteem (yes, I am still attractive to the opposite sex, despite being celibate for more than a year) or the necessary rebound momentum (the ex is no longer the last guy you slept with) – and leave it at that.

DO be in control

From choosing the location to calling it a night, make sure it's you who's calling the shots. Stay in control – if you're completely smashed, it's best just to take his number and get a cab home. Take heed of the example set by Monique: ignore the moral of this story at your peril. She and Gavin went out for dinner before she took him back to her place for something that wasn't exactly on the menu. Fuelled by nerves and the best part of a couple of bottles of wine (not to mention those vodkas in the bar before dinner), Monique was decidedly the worse for wear by the time the rumpy-pumpy started. Still, Gavin seemed quite happy so she lay back, thought of England and tried not to feel too queasy as the motion got going. Job done (thankfully, it didn't last too long), they dozed off to sleep. But when Gavin awoke, it wasn't quite the post-coital cuddle he'd been dreaming of. Instead, Monique had thrown up everywhere. The sheets, her hair, Gavin: everything was covered in half-digested peri-peri chicken. Apparently Gavin – despite the name – had quite a fit body as he was a surfer, but Monique wasn't destined to ride any more waves with him. The verdict, officially, was 'wipeout'. As far as we're concerned, the only time you should be out of control on a one-night stand is on the point of orgasm.

DON'T forget to lock the bedroom door

We know what it's like, the cab ride home was a whirlwind of wandering hands and now you're home the passion has obliterated all common sense.

But remember this tip at least. From friends to flatmates, fellow holidaymakers to cleaning staff, the last thing you want is for your 'Ohhhh' to be transformed into: 'Oh, no. Bugger, we forgot to lock the door,' as you're rudely interrupted in flagrante by any of the aforementioned folk. Chris and Ellie were friends who got it on when a group of mates all took a holiday to Majorca. The chemistry became too much one night as everyone was gathering in the lobby to go clubbing. Chris and Ellie, who'd lingered behind as everyone was locking up, were squeezing in a quickie when a friend nipped back to the room for her forgotten camera. Suffice to say, the frisky couple weren't quite in the mood to say 'Cheese!' at the time ... though both did have huge smiles on their faces just a short time later.

12 DO be aware of your belongings at all times

This applies especially if you've taken him back to yours. The man in question may seem solvent, even loaded, but appearances can always be deceptive. If you've dozed off, do you really know what he was doing while you slept? Sadly, Adele took this tip to extremes when she pulled a Moroccan fitness trainer one crazy Christmas (his name has been lost in the mists of time). Having had her fill of his terrifically toned body, Adele drifted off to sleep (well, passed out and woke herself with a snore). The fitness trainer was up, dressed and clearly ready to leave. Adele, on the ball as ever, did some quick thinking (tinged with only a little paranoia), and insisted that he return her wallet, which she couldn't see anywhere. He denied all knowledge of the dastardly theft, but Adele was not to be swayed. The room was searched: no wallet. 'Where is it?' she demanded. 'I don't have it,' he said. 'Honestly.' She reasoned in reply, 'Well, I had it when I came home, and it's not here now.' She stared him down: 'Lift up your arms.' At this point, the Moroccan is subjected to a pat-down security search courtesy of the drunken Adele. 'Turn,' she commands. The search continues. No wallet. Bugger. 'It must be here somewhere,' she says, 'and you're not leaving until I find it.' Half an hour later, a sheepish Adele locates the recalcitrant wallet at the bottom of her wardrobe – it had been shoved in the cupboard along with the dirty washing when the unexpected pull necessitated a quick-fire clean-up of the bedroom. 'You can go now,' she relents. 'Can I see you again?' he requests. (Amazingly, he was still interested even after Adele had just accused him of theft – she must have been good, is all we can say.) 'Most certainly not,' replied this modern-day Miss Marple, and with that she showed him the door.

DO feel comfortable with whatever is going on

One-night stands can be opportunities to try new things – there's every chance you're not going to see this man ever again (if that's the way you want to play it), so this may well be the time to act out fantasies you'd never confess to in your everyday life. Relish the footloose freedom that your relative anonymity gives you. Enjoy your night – and remember, if you're not happy with what's going on, put a stop to it immediately. Don't forget, too, that there are certain shenanigans a woman should avoid at all costs:

Sex Games You Should Never Agree To

• Bondage using handcuffs which require real keys. Do you trust him to unlock them when it's all over and, perhaps more importantly, not to lose the keys? (Men can be so absent-minded – and how would you explain that predicament come Monday morning at the office?)

• Role-playing as an innocent 1950s housewife. Trust us: it's just an excuse to get you to do his washing-up. He may burst into the kitchen a bit later on, dressed as a plumber and all set to ravish you on the kitchen table – but he'll only ever make his move after the dishes are done. You have been warned.

• Making use of chocolate body paint and/or whipped cream ... unless he's volunteering to do the laundry. Five hours spent scrubbing soiled sheets really does take the shine off any sexiness which might have been initially involved.

• Attempting sexual acrobatics that a professional gymnast would be hard-pushed to pull off. Some positions should only ever be endeavoured after a full body warm-up – and even then staged only in a safe, controlled environment, with an expert on hand for advice and the St John's Ambulance volunteers standing by in case of injury.

So, what happens next? Sadly, as we all know, some men are simply after a fleeting fumble (or four) and nothing more: we've all got the emotional scars to prove that. We hope, if it is a case of 'sayonara before sunrise', that you won't have got yourself too emotionally involved at this early stage. All the same, it still hurts like hell to find that your man is married / attached (funny how it's only afterwards that their partners come into the conversation); or just plain uninterested, before you've even put your clothes back on. But such is life. If you've taken the attitude that you're just out for a good time too, it can be a mutually satisfying situation, without a single shattered soul. His decision to move on suits you fine: at least you can get a bit of proper kip before the day starts.

However, for every player there will be a man who wants to take things further (and, we think, understandably, after the sexual prowess you have, in all likelihood, rather recently displayed). How you respond to these overtures depends on how you feel about the man under consideration. Is he a stallion in the sack – or was the whole thing a bit more like a donkey ride in Devon?

Before making your decision about whether to see him again, also consider carefully, where do you see this leading? Sometimes it's preferable to keep these stop-gap shags separate from the search for Mr Right. After all, meeting a man when you're dressed in a PVC catsuit and are more enthusiastic than a contestant on *Celebrity Love Island* gives a slightly misleading impression of the more everyday you:

librarian for the primary school reading centre, and staunch social pillar of your local community. He might expect whips and chains for the rest of his days, but if you're more concerned with organizing the upcoming Enid Blyton Appreciation Festival, would this really work long term? If your one-nighter has been a night for the fantasy life but not for the future, it's probably best to kill it right now, or you'll be failing to meet expectations every time you pull on a pair of trainers rather than your thigh-high boots.

Case Study: Jody

She found herself in an impossible situation after a one-night stand. Her fling with Russell had been the stuff of legend – multiple orgasms, multiple positions ... but it left her with the problem of a multiple personality. When the venue changed from the bedroom to a bar, the girl who talked dirty wasn't quite so comfortable talking about herself, and as for Russell, he simply wondered what had happened to the crazy woman with the one-track mind – it seemed she could actually think outside her box after all, what a disappointment. As Jody discovered, it's one thing to play the femme fatale for a single evening, but it's a role that can't seriously be maintained for life.

On the other hand, however, you pulled this guy because you fancied him. So who's to say that underneath the superficial attraction there isn't a deeper connection to the soul? (Or at the very least, an ability to hold a conversation with each other which lasts a little longer than 'Get your coat, you've pulled.') If you are making moves on each other because the prospects are promising, it begs the question: how far do you go when you take him home? Bear in mind that Peter Andre twice had a hit with 'Mysterious Girl' – there is something to be said for not revealing all the moment that you meet. Just because you've gone home with a guy, there's really no pressure to go all the way. Sometimes the best nights are when you leave each other wanting more...

Case Study: Beth and Lara

These lovely ladies met a couple of very nice gentlemen while queuing for a club one night. The guys were friends and flatmates and the foursome really hit it off, with Beth pairing up with Ed while Lara liked Marcus. Post-dancing, Lara and Beth both went back to the lads' for a nightcap. After talking until the early hours, the couples then retired to respective bedrooms – Lara and Marcus slept together, but Beth and Ed did not. The next morning Ed asked for Beth's number, but there was a resounding silence from Mr Marcus. He wasn't interested in seeing Lara again: for him it was just a one-night stand.

Happily for Beth, however, Ed called within the week and the pair started dating. When asked, Ed said that he would still have called even if they had slept together the night they met, but we'll never know if that actually would have happened. Ultimately, Beth felt that Ed respected her more for holding back, and she enjoyed the fact that their sexual relationship then developed as their emotional intimacy did. Delayed gratification is perhaps the way forward if there's to be a future in a fling.

So, it is possible to date someone when you've gone home with them the same night you met. Getting naked with and then getting to know a man is not the ideal scenario if you're looking for a relationship – but it can work out. Hey, if the sexual chemistry was so strong that you couldn't resist each other, at least you know the affair will be passionate, even if it finally fails to fulfil potential.

Simply put, when it comes to one-night wonders, be safe, know what you want out of the experience and – as Kylie Minogue once sang, way back in 1989 – enjoy yourself. From strictly orgasmic encounters to sowing the seeds of something more serious, we hope that either way it's a night just full of naughtiness.

Let Me Entertain You

Y ou may have just spent the night with him; or your eyes might have met across a crowded room. He could be your friend, a sexy stranger, your Internet chum, or your best mate's brother. However it happened, we hope by now you will have met a man who is at least a Mr Worth Pursuing. But, with that first hurdle over, the next is even more daunting: your first date together.

Like the first time you ever have sex, losing your date virginity with a man can be awkward, uncomfortable, and not a little messy. Like sex, it will either be an orgasmic experience or just an immense disappointment. First dates can comprise the classic drinks-and-dinner evening date, a lunchtime picnic, a wander round an art gallery, a movie ... or even a trip to the zoo (yes, you did read that correctly – and for the record the girl concerned wasn't ten years old at the time, she was twenty-three, and had a great time). For traditionalists, however, the drinks-dinner-movie combo is the triple bill to triumph every time.

The initial date is an odd and potentially anxious affair. So much is dependent on these first impressions that you can feel under more pressure than the seat of Rik Waller's pants. Remember, however – as with that old adage about job interviews – that your man is under as much scrutiny from you as you are from him. You're both simply trying one another out to see how things fit. On occasion it will be a case of hand-me-down hell – not long enough where it counts and lacking in material where it matters most – but on the other hand your rapport could be like slipping into your favourite and most seductive bra – comfortable, sexy and full of support.

What to wear?

Perhaps the single most important question you will ask yourself all evening. Obviously, planning what to wear is tantamount to a military operation. The key is to look fantastic but to do so in a way that doesn't look like you have spent hours trying (even though you have). Inevitably, nothing in your wardrobe will seem right for the occasion, and an emergency assault on the high street appears essential. Remember, however, that the blessed thing about a first date is that he's likely only ever to have seen you in one outfit before. Brilliant: whatever you wear will suggest that you always look this great (after all, he doesn't need to know about those 'at home' clothes just yet...). If your date has developed from a long-term friendship, remember that this is, after all, a man – so you're pretty safe in assuming

that you could wear anything and he wouldn't know if he'd seen it before. Prior to spending your pennies on six new outfits catering for all weather conditions (plus accessories), scrutinize your current clothing options with care – there may well be something suitable already in your wardrobe.

Obviously, your outfit selection will depend on the venue and planned activities. Do find out beforehand what the plan of action is so that you will be appropriately attired for the occasion. Whatever the date, though, don't go OTT (unless in fact you are accompanying him to a black-tie ball). The first-date outfit should look understated, chic, sexy and subtle as opposed to a desperately-trying-to-impress ensemble. You may well own a gorgeous Ben de Lisi gown that makes you look a million dollars (and has been worn only once before at your graduation ceremony eight years ago), but this is not the time to show him your red-carpet credentials. Instead, think low-key, think casual, and most importantly think comfortable. We're not talking trackie bottoms and trainers (unless a run in the park is the order of the day), but rather an outfit in which you feel like yourself, and about which you won't worry during the date. (VPL, anyone? Does my bum look big in this?) Wear something in which you feel attractive and we guarantee that you will knock him dead. Make sure you feel comfortable in your clothes and you will feel all the more confident within (that might sound a tad American-chat-show, but trust us – it is true).

Similarly, in your aim to attract him, don't be too enthusiastic on the sexual side of things: cleavage doesn't always equal conquest. Yes, he loves breasts, but they may well put him off his steak if they're presented with more trimmings than the meal itself. You're also setting yourself up for an evening of him talking to your chest all night, rather than to you – and we imagine you'd like him to know a little more about you than just your cup size by the time he takes you home.

✆ Case Study: Rebecca

She thought her date was taking her somewhere 'nice' for dinner, so appropriately wore a little black dress. However, the man in question clearly had very different ideas about what constituted a 'nice' restaurant: by the time the words 'Wetherspoons' and 'two meals for a fiver' were mentioned, the dress somehow no longer seemed like the correct outfit. LBD and HP Sauce just don't mix.

Pride and punctuality

While a date rendezvous doesn't strictly require the timekeeping accuracy of a metronome, it is important to be roughly punctual on the first date. If you can. Obviously hair disasters, last-minute wardrobe changes, railway engineering works and the weather all conspire against you at times like these, but at least your heart will be in the right place. Text or call him if you're going to be late – it's only fair. Pity Ian, who was left waiting for forty-five minutes outside the Odeon when Gemma was running late. She called, got a cab, got lost, phoned for directions, got lost again, and eventually arrived to meet him an hour and a half after they'd scheduled. The movie was a write-off, the date pretty much the same a short time later, perhaps predictably so.

Of course, sometimes the shoe is on the other foot. What to do if your date is late? If you're in a bar, order a drink and get comfortable. Wait for him while you have a Screaming Orgasm – women are so great at multi-tasking – and if you haven't heard from him after that, leave. Wait for twenty minutes max for a visible date or at least a telephonic update, otherwise put him down as a no-show. Well, you'll show him. No point in wasting such a fabulous outfit – hit the town and go dancing with your mates instead.

The venue

Your first impression of him. Where has he taken you? Somewhere classy, pricey, cosy, romantic … or McDonald's? Hopefully you will have mentioned any dietary needs to him beforehand and you're not stuck in a fish restaurant if you're allergic to seafood – a near-death experience followed by a four-hour wait at A&E for antihistamine treatment is not our idea of a great night out. Observe how he behaves in the place. Do the staff know him? Does he even

consult the menu? Players often take their first dates to the same restaurant each time – and while we all have favourite venues, a lady likes to feel that a special effort has been made on her behalf. Jenny, a veggie, found that her man had trawled the Internet, joined a debate forum at work and consulted his vegetarian brother before deciding on their date venue: the extra effort earned him brownie points right from the start.

Pace yourself

Dates can be nerve-racking experiences. Whatever you do, avoid the temptation to stock up on Dutch courage. Even if the conversation is initially stilted, don't neck your drink in those pregnant pauses. If the date takes a while to get going, you could find that you've downed an entire bottle of wine before you've even ordered. Know your limitations – while some us can drink three bottles of vino and still sound relatively sober, others of us are under the table midway through the second G&T. Stick to water or non-alcoholic cocktails if you're ever in doubt. And remember that well-known (but not frequently adhered to) little gem of advice: for every alcoholic drink, consume a glass of water to go with it. Your head will thank you for it in the morning.

If only Justin had followed such advice. Ruth was horrified when, on her date with this seemingly well-turned-out young man, he proceeded to do his utmost to give the young George Best a run for his money. Justin wasn't drinking like a fish, he was drinking for the whole shoal. He brought new meaning to the phrase 'pre-dinner drinks'. The date was over by half past eight, by which point he had passed out and Ruth had pissed off.

Similarly, Tara insists to this day that if she hadn't drunk two bottles of pink champagne on an empty stomach, she would never have gone to bed with Johnny – a man twelve years her senior, by several leagues inferior (if she was Premiership, he was fighting relegation from the Nationwide Conference), and he had a hairy back to boot. It just goes to show, you should always pace yourself on dates – or you may not ever live down the consequences.

Decisions, decisions...

Hmm, what to eat at dinner. We are most definitely of the 'don't be coy' school – we're not saying order the most expensive thing on the menu, but if you're starving and fancy a starter, there's no need to deny yourself a bit of garlic bread (though, in that instance, do make sure he's having the same). Also, eat properly. Why order just a starter-sized salad (no dressing), if you know you're going to end up in the all-night garage five hours on, scoffing Pringles and eating chocolate bars to 'get your sugar levels up'? (More likely, to satiate your extreme hunger, as you missed lunch due to a last-minute panic over nail varnish.) It's far, far better to have a normal, healthy meal than attempt to seduce him with your ability to nibble a single lettuce leaf for an entire hour. Besides which, a) he won't have noticed whether you've eaten or not, so your endeavour to be 'dainty' will have utterly passed him by, and b) the loud rumblings of your hungry tummy are really not the ideal soundtrack to seduction. As always, post-meal, check your appearance for any embarrassing spillages, unintentional chin decorations and, of course, any food caught between your teeth (never a good look, especially if it's spinach).

A little more conversation

The first date is when the two of you get to know a little more about each other, whatever the history of your attraction. Careers, music tastes, families, living arrangements, passions, dreams and ambitions are all fair game – but maybe lay off the relationship histories and sexual CVs for the time being (you never know what the 'ex files' might reveal, and although the truth is out there, quite frankly sometimes that's where it should stay). Don't be alarmed at occasional lulls in conversation (after all, you've got to eat sometime – think of them as comfortable silences), but if you find yourself purely discussing the weather – and that only sporadically – it's pretty much a foregone conclusion that this date won't see a sequel (and thank God!).

Sophie found her first-date conversation with one bloke a real eye-opener. She'd met him at a university reunion party, and had told all her friends about this amazing fellow graduate she'd found. He'd studied psychology, was a like-minded mountaineering enthusiast and came from Manchester – it was all perfect. Imagine her surprise, therefore, to discover on their date that he was in fact a) from South Africa, b) afraid of heights, c) not a graduate, and d) more psycho than psychology student. Quite how she'd got him so wrong at their initial meeting is (officially) unknown – but we think a '2 for 1' deal on Smirnoff Ice that night may well have had something to do with it.

Going Dutch?

Not a mini-break to Holland, of course, but whether or not you split the bill. Feminist theories aside, we ourselves are traditionalists and would always opt for him to pay outright – after all, he is the one taking you out, not vice versa. However, we would also recommend that you pay for some aspect of the evening – a round of drinks, a cab fare, etc. Dinner and any tickets are perhaps best left to him, if he's offering to pay. Don't forget to take money with you, though – whether for an emergency getaway or for spoiling him rotten (if the date's that good), it's always best to have your financial independence, just in case.

Annie had a horrendous experience on one first date.

Having spent the day with Paul, who had bored her rotten dragging her to various historical sites of 'interest' (apparently), she wanted nothing more than to go home and drown her sorrows in a G&T and a hot bath. However, Paul insisted on taking her out for a slap-up meal, to thank her for a 'great' day (yeah, right) and to treat her, as she was a student without any cash. They settled into an extremely posh restaurant, ordered expensive wine and multiple courses, and were settling back with liqueurs when Paul handed over his credit card to settle the three-digit bill. 'Sir, a problem...' The waiter interrupts to advise that the card payment is not going through. Paul hands over another card. 'Sir...' It's the waiter again. Paul smiles at Annie, gesticulates apology and humble pie, and it slowly dawns on her that he is expecting her to pay, which she cannot afford to do. As she begrudgingly hands over her already maxed-out credit card, Paul neatly folds his napkin, gets up from his chair, and confidently strides out of the restaurant without a backward glance. By the time Annie has signed for the meal and emerged on to the street behind him, he is nowhere to be seen, and five angry voicemails don't elicit a single apology, explanation or response from him. Still, at least she wasn't left with the washing-up.

Hold me, thrill me, kiss me

Ah, that first date dilemma of 'How far do we go?' From

the very start of your date, whatever the previous circumstances, we think it best to think chaste and think cheeks. Even if you were snogging each other's faces off the night before, the fact that you are now on a date puts the liaison on an entirely different level. Take a step back from any former intimacy – at least until you've decided that, actually, your man radar is on fire even when you are drunk, and my God you've made a good pull. By all means kiss when you greet, but perhaps proffer your cheek coquettishly instead of having a full tongue sarnie, even if he initiates the latter.

At the end of the date, well, it could be all or nothing. The night might end abruptly if it's been that bad (in which case, there's always 'work the next day' or an imperative 'early rise' to use as your infallible get-out cards). For Shannon and Rob, they parted amicably and with delicious potential after their first date – but without a single kiss, for that happened on their second (once Rob had lost his nerves and Shannon knew where she stood). On occasion, delayed gratification is *so* the way forward … and those two certainly made up for lost time. Some women are of the school of thought that holding out means holding on to a man – but the jury's still out on that one, and the evidence is far from conclusive.

Alternatively, you can go 'full on' immediately after the first date. As long as it feels right for you, it's probably the right thing to do. Follow your instincts. But remember – just because you kiss him, it doesn't necessarily mean that he has to come back to yours for 'coffee'. And just because he comes back to yours for 'coffee', it doesn't necessarily mean that you have any in...

Slow

o, the first date's over. You're not yet sure if he's your Mr Right, but you'd certainly like to take things further. The next step is 'thank you' – always polite to say after any date, but it's also the perfect excuse to keep in contact with him, particularly if you're still not sure where it all might lead. If the first date hasn't given you enough to go on in order to come to a decision about whether you're right together or not, a second date is an absolute must. For Mary, her follow-up date with Mike unfortunately proved that there was not a jot of chemistry between them. He, however, thought otherwise, and had taken her to a stunning rooftop restaurant for their second date. It was both extortionate and excruciating, set as it was in one of the most romantic places Mary had ever seen. Nevertheless, despite the key location, location, location, Mike simply didn't pass the surveyor's report – and Mary was back on the market.

If the second date *is* a success, you've got a real

contender on your hands, and more importantly, in your arms. How to avoid falling at the first hurdle? Some girls think a third date means you're meant to be, but we think it's better to take things slowly – at least, don't mention marriage and kids yet. Here's a brief guide to what not to do in the early stages:

Don't match your name to his to see what would happen if you married

Yes, we've all done it, but there's certainly no need to tell him about it, and if you've been practising your married signature for God's sake don't leave your doodles lying about. He won't think it's sweet; he'll scarper. Remember not to pick out your kids' names either – there's getting ahead of yourself, and there's shooting yourself in the foot. This is an example of both.

Don't push for commitment – you're in the early stages

From booking up all his weekends for the next six months to dropping 'subtle' hints about engagements, it's all too much too soon. Don't be needy and demand to spend all your time together – after all, this will simply reveal your faults to him just that little bit sooner. Keep your air of mystery and you'll keep him hooked.

Don't make him choose between his mates and you

Chances are you'll end up second best, and then you'll really know where you stand: out in the cold.

Don't 'show him off'
You may be triumphant in securing a man and keen to parade him before your friends and family, but he's unlikely to appreciate the 'show-and-tell' sessions. By blowing your own trumpet you could blow it completely.

Don't try to put a label on him
After all, he's not a jar of your mum's home-made chutney. In fact, the only pickle around will be the one you get yourself into if you try to rush things. We know how difficult it can be to define a relationship, and that knowing where you stand with a man can be a frequent issue, but remember

that making each other happy is always much more important than making things 'official'.

However, dating isn't all about what not to do (and we're no big fans of the Trinny-and-Susannah negative mentality anyway). So here are some tips for the kind of approach you *should* be taking. Not only will these steps allow you to enjoy the blossoming relationship, they will demonstrate that you can still be independent … meaning the chances of a(nother) broken heart are next to nil. With odds like that, surely it's worth taking a gamble?

Step 1.
Retain your independent life
∙∙

Keep up any commitments, line up line-dancing sessions with pals (or just meet them down the pub – Steps' '5,6,7,8' hasn't quite reached world-domination stage yet), and most importantly don't let the new relationship overpower your social life. Sure, it's great to see him, but small doses are often the best way to take both medicine and men. Make sure you hold on to the life you had BB (Before Boyfriend) and you'll both be happier for it.

Step 2.
Be footloose and fancy free
∙∙

Just because you've hit it off with one guy, don't burn your bridges with any other shining knights. If you're not exclusively dating someone (and you'll have a sense of whether you are or not), *do* accept other dates and keep your eyes peeled for pulling possibilities. Men especially will be taking this approach, so why shouldn't you?

Step 3.
Leave the analysis to the psychotherapists

· ·

There's nothing more off-putting on a date than an inner running commentary all about it. 'Hmm, I liked the way he held the door open for me. But, oh dear, he smokes. Not sure I could spend the rest of my life with someone who smokes...' Analysing everything he does and says, in order to determine whether there is a future in the relationship, is perhaps the one thing almost certain to ensure that there is none. Just relax and enjoy your dates. Have fun. Relish his company and cherish the attention. Don't forget, too, that if you're busy concentrating on your stream-of-consciousness inner monologue, you may miss him mentioning any number of important things that you really need to know about him –
for example, his obsession with fungal growths; his desire for a family of at least nine children; his multimillion-pound annual salary, his Michelin-starred culinary skills...

Step 4.
Be cautious

This applies even if you do think he's The One. For, after all, *if* he is, a month or so of you tempering your tenderness will hardly put him off, and he'll still be around once you're ready to commit more fully. On the other hand, if after the honeymoon period vanishes he does too, you won't have given him your heart and soul to sacrifice. Use your survival instincts. Esther, even though she could feel herself falling for her new man, held back a little. She only saw him at weekends to start with, and even then would see her friends for some other outing too. Little by little, she came to trust her man and found that their strong feelings for each other were truly mutual. Only then did she throw caution to the wind and commit to a weekend away. (Mini-breaking is *so* the way forward. Self-preservation has a lot to be said for it, too.)

Step 5.
Take it slow

As the saying goes, fools rush in. With the sex, the bill-sharing, meeting friends and family, leaving a toothbrush at his flat … remember that nothing has to happen overnight.

If this is going to work out, you will have all the time in the world for every single aspect of your shenanigans. So savour the early stages. George Michael may have had a number one with 'Fast Love', but 'I Will Always Love You' is one of the biggest-selling songs of all time. There's something in that, you know.

We trust that following these pointers will lead to your long-term happiness. At the very least, you won't have scared him off with any semblance of a Glenn Close impression: well done you. As ever, we think success in seduction is primarily down to retaining some self-esteem. So as long as you don't go all puppy-dog on him (at least until he's prepared to rub your belly for all time), and as long as you are focusing on the fact that he *complements* rather than *completes* you – well, then you'll be doing yourself proud.

Perhaps, Perhaps, Perhaps

Things are going well. You've had more than a few dates, you've confessed to your feelings for each other – hey, well done, you've got yourself a long-term boyfriend. NB: By our definition, 'long-term' is anything over three months (it's what's called setting ourselves achievable goals). In fact, it's often said that there is a 'three-month rule' – if a couple are still loved-up after that first trimester, chances are they may well stay the course. But how do you know if he really is The One? What are the telltale signs that tell you this is the man for you?

6 Everything inside you is telling you he's right

From the way you feel in his arms to the way he makes you laugh, your whole relationship is based on a natural connection that doesn't require embellishment or enforced effort. There are absolutely no games – you love and trust each other and are totally secure in the strength of your relationship. It may have happened from the very start, or maybe after you were together for a while, but inside, in your very marrow, you simply know the two of you are right together: he is your One.

You feel entirely comfortable with him

We're not necessarily talking snuggles on the squishy sofa here, or even being completely happy with him seeing you naked (in our experience, if the latter was truly an indicator of finding Mr Right, 'The One' wouldn't really be an accurate description of that special someone). Rather, when you're with him there is absolutely no pressure. No pressure to be anything other than yourself. You don't have to be witty, gorgeous or good company (even though you're invariably all three, all of the time); you don't have to be the career woman, the sex symbol or the domestic goddess – instead, you're just plain old you, and safe in the knowledge that he loves you for it.

∞ Somehow, he has become your best friend

He might not paint your toenails or appreciate the fine art of shopping for shoes, but he is always the person to whom you tell things first; your successes, your traumas, and the trivia of your day-to-day life – and, amazingly, he listens and he cares. When you tell him you've been promoted, he's more excited than you are. When you mention you're feeling a bit under the weather, he orders strict bed rest and chicken soup, while he goes out to buy the finest pharmaceutical remedies Boots has to offer. (OK, so maybe all boyfriends aren't quite this attentive, but you get the gist.)

✒ You still can't get enough of each other

You've been together for a while – and yet he can still take your breath away and make you tremble at the knees (not to mention a few other, rather more significant places). Sexually, you're in tune with each other and consistently hit all the right notes – Pavarotti is not a patch on your passion. Even better, there's still uncharted territory to discover and, hell, you're having a damn good time doing just that.

✒ You have the best fun together

Never has simply going to Sainsbury's been quite so enjoyable: browsing the aisles, going through the checkout, teaching each other your idiosyncratic bag-packing techniques – the whole experience overlaid with much laughter, jollity and snogs next to the olive oil (not so much a taste of Italy as a taste of each other). When you're with Mr Right, practically everything you do together is the best fun you've had since the last time you met (cleaning the bathroom an obvious exception). He has transformed your everyday life from the mundane to the marvellous. When the two of you are alone together, it's like the rest of the world fades away and the world is only each other (God, doesn't it make you sick?).

⑨ You don't mind compromising to make him happy

We're not saying you should roll over each time there's a confrontation, just to let him have his way (though, in our experience, 'rolling over to let him have his way' can lead to a hell of a lot of fun…), but, rather, you find that sacrificing the small things to make him happy actually makes you really happy too (and vice versa). You willingly give things up for each other, from smoking, to control of the TV remote, to your very last Rolo. That's true love.

⑩ You have no fear of your future

Though the specifics aren't mapped out, the two of you know you will be together for a very long time to come. (NB: Here we are talking longer than just another three months!) You openly admit to wanting to share your lives together, and look forward to supporting one another in whatever the years may throw at you. Simply put, you can't imagine your life without him in it.

But what happens if you're feeling none of the above, but are still with someone you thought was Mr Right? Could it be that he is, after all, just another Mr Wrong? We all fall head over heels at times, and listen to our hearts rather than our heads – your better judgement helpfully takes a sabbatical on some relationships – but, always, there comes a time when you have to ask yourself, Is he really The One? Maybe the following case studies might shed some light on why 'Mr Right' doesn't always live up to his name.

Case Study 1: Fergus

Fergus and Kirsty met at university – surely the place, she thought, to find her future husband: not only do millions of people meet their life partners there, but Kirsty's parents and sisters had all tied the knot with fellow graduates (talk about pressure, poor girl). On paper, Fergus seemed like the perfect man – he and Kirsty were into the same things, he was charming, good-looking and intelligent, and he got on well with her parents. Surely it was a match made in heaven? For a year and a half, Kirsty convinced herself that this was the case. But in her heart, she knew he wasn't The One. For a start, and unbeknownst to Fergus, he was the spitting image of the love of Kirsty's life – a man who broke her heart when she was seventeen. For Kirsty, her relationship with Fergus was a replay of that former love – but this time, with a happy ending that she was determined to make happen (even if it killed her). And therein lay the second problem: if Fergus was Mr Right, no effort was needed to make those dreams come true. As it was, Kirsty – to be frank – manipulated the entire relationship, driven by her resolution to make Fergus The One. But if you're forcing it, it's doomed to fail. And despite their apparent compatibility on the surface, Kirsty and Fergus were just not right together. Fergus 'ticked all the boxes', but Mr Right can't be identified simply through drawing up a list of quantifiable criteria (must be at least six foot; must love chocolate; must do DIY): he's got to have that 'X' factor, that 'wow' factor. If he's got it, he's got your heart … but if he hasn't, he's just got to go.

Case Study 2: Tim

Tim and Eve went out for three years, a relationship that was complicated (or, according to Eve, strengthened) by the fact that Tim worked in America and Eve lived in England. They barely saw each other, but maintained that 'absence makes the heart grow fonder'. However, for Tim it was more 'out of sight, out of mind'. Rumours of his casual infidelity filtered through from mutual friends, but Eve fell foul of the fantasy trap, projecting her desires for the perfect boyfriend on to the absent Tim. She saw him so infrequently that she was able to build him up in her head as the ideal partner – and he wasn't around to contradict her daydreams. Problems arose, however, when he moved to the UK: living in the same city wasn't quite the sexy scenario Eve had imagined. Tim, to her horror, turned out to be nothing like the boyfriend she'd thought she had. In fact, Tim was the same man he'd always been, Eve just couldn't kid herself any more when the evidence was right in front of her … Tim just wasn't her Mr Right.

Sometimes, the wrong men slip through the net or, for whatever reason, your new relationship just doesn't cut the mustard. It's not working out, for either of you. It's always best to face the facts about this early on rather than burying your head in the sand. The harsh but simple truth is, if he's not calling or replying to texts, or keeps rearranging dates saying he's really busy at work, he's losing interest. In short, to cite the now infamous line from *Sex and the City*, he's just not that into you. Don't feel bad about it, but learn to recognize the signs early on so that you can bring things to an end before you waste any more time on yet another Mr Wrong. Check out our 'Countdown to Catastrophe' – if you notice any of the following symptoms, your relationship's in seriously poor health:

⑥ Lack of communication

Whereas once you ran up phone bills that kept BT in business, these days you're lucky if you get a text message once a week.

Out of sight, out of mind

He may be utterly attentive when he's on a date with you, but in between times he's like the Invisible Man. It's always you phoning to arrange the next date: if this is the case, alarm bells should be ringing.

Backtracking

Men can scare themselves off sometimes. They wade in with declarations of affection but later panic that they've got themselves in too deep. Suddenly, they were 'really drunk' and 'can't remember a thing they said', or you're responsible for taking things too fast (even though he was the one discussing colour schemes for the nursery you'll have in five years' time). If he's not man enough to stand by his emotions, he's not man enough for you.

Wandering eyes

Recently, when you've been on dates together, your drop-dead gorgeous outfits (not to mention scintillating conversation) are no longer quite enough to hold his attention. You've noticed that his eyes are always focused somewhere over your shoulder: he's looking for his next pull. On occasion, the man who's losing interest will go to even greater lengths to find fresh prey – while stringing you along at the very same time, of course. Sue, having dated Richard for over a year, was horrified when one of her single friends informed her that they'd spotted Richard's photo on an Internet dating site. Not content with having a long-term relationship, Richard was seeing other women on the side and billing himself as 'available' on the website's helpful biog. Funnily enough, his relationship with Sue didn't get a mention, though he made sure to reveal his love of watersports, affection for small animals, and – naturally – his tireless charity work with autistic children. According to his 'user rating', he was quite the catch. It all smelt decidedly fishy to Sue. Time to move on: frankly, she had bigger (that being the operative word) fish to fry.

Can't pin him down

And we're not talking voodoo here (though there's a thought...). No matter which day you suggest for meeting up, he's always got plans – even three weeks in advance. This smacks of a man weaselling his way out of an actual break-up confrontation. Chloë was once 'finished with' via a text message, which said quite simply 'Can't make Wed'. As the man in question couldn't even be bothered to write the day in full, what hope was there that he would ever fully commit? Sometimes it's worth you taking the initiative and putting an actual stop to the relationship; although men would often rather things just petered out, without either one of you ever saying anything (countless relationships have died a death this way), we feel it's always best to have closure.

Natalie agreed, and when her man started being shifty and elusive about dates, she phoned him up to say she didn't want to see him again – he was a lovely guy (not), it just wasn't working for her. She was left with the upper hand and the satisfaction of knowing she dumped him, while he was left reaching for those man-sized tissues (and on that note, let's leave it there – men and tissues is a combination with entirely different connotations from that of women and tears).

Occasionally, men can be a bit more direct. Here are five ways to tell if you're a turn-off (all taken from real life!). If he springs any of the following on you, it's unlikely the pair of you will see the hour out together, let alone the evening:

How To Tell If You're A Turn-Off

'I'd love to ask you back, but I'm at a key stage in my marathon training and I need to get seven hours' sleep.'

'I'm afraid I need to concentrate on my audit exam.'
(NB: It is advisable only ever to date *qualified* accountants.)

'I've got a lot on at work at the moment.'

Scenario: snuggled up on the sofa with a DVD. He explains: 'I can't stay for the whole movie, I've got to go home and do my ironing.'

'I'm really sorry but I just don't fancy you.'

Exchanges You Never Want To Hear In Bed

Him: So, are you dating anyone else?

You: No, I wouldn't while I'm seeing you. Would you?

(At this point, a long pause follows and you know you're in trouble.)

Him: Actually, yes. There's no one else I'd rather go out with at the moment – but if that changes I'll let you know.

Him: Have you got any credit on your phone? I need to call my mum to tell her I won't be home...

Either of you: What was your name again?

Him: So where's your boyfriend tonight?

You: Well, as I'm in bed with you, obviously I don't have one.

(An awkward moment in which you know what's coming.)

You: So where's your girlfriend?

Him: Erm, back home in bed.

You: You're serious, aren't you?

Him: Actually, yes, we've been living together for four years.

You: So what the hell are you doing here?

Him: Well I really like you. And my relationship's going through a bad patch. My girlfriend just doesn't understand me.

But, as we advised back in the first chapter, a break-up really doesn't mean a breakdown. Think of it more as a liberating experience, and compare it to the fashion world – your ex was just *so* last season, and you're now looking forward to checking out the latest models on the catwalk instead. Just as a winter coat would be hugely inappropriate for sexy summer days, so your love life needs freshening up every now and again. It really isn't shattering – it's potentially sensational. Whoever prompts the moving on, simply make sure it's you who gets on with the moving on up.

Leave Right Now

Despite the clichés, it's not always the female of the species who is full-on in a fling. Women certainly don't hold exclusive rights in the OTT stakes when it comes to commitment. It's an alarming development when the man in your life is suddenly too keen – you may think it would be a dream come true, but believe us when we say it's a nightmare.

Roddy, for example, seemed like an ordinary down-to-earth guy. Helen went on a date with him and was rather impressed – he was friendly, funny, courteous and didn't play games. The offer of a second date was made swiftly and without embarrassment. Delighted, she accepted. Theirs was a summer fling, and when Roddy mentioned that a friend was having a barbecue, it seemed like the perfect casual second date. Oh, how wrong can you be. On arrival, Helen met the only other couple in attendance – and they'd been together for years. A drink in hand, she learned that the barbecue was in fact an intimate birthday celebration for one of Roddy's closest friends; she felt slightly uncomfortable at accompanying him to such a personal gathering. By the time they ate, Roddy was describing her as his girlfriend, and his arm seemed surgically attached to her waist. Helen left before dessert – the possibility that the pavlova could come with a proposal was frighteningly real.

Similarly, Liz got a shock when, having seen a guy once, she began receiving daily emails from him regarding their astrological compatibility – complete with horoscope analysis and predictions in each missive. He seemed to think that they were written in the stars – her first priority was to write him out of her life.

However, sometimes this is easier said than done. At times men just don't get the message. You've been polite, you have declined dates – and yet he keeps calling. If you don't answer the phone right away, you receive five text messages to check you're still alive. At first you take the calls and explain yet again that you don't want to see him. Surely his self-respect will kick in at this point and this will be the last you hear from him? Unfortunately not. The calls continue, at all hours of the day and night. He starts withholding his number in the hope that you will pick up. When that doesn't work he develops a nasty habit of leaving silent voicemails – by now the term 'bunny boiler' is too good for him. Enough is enough, so what do you do next?

What To Do If He Becomes Your Stalker

. . . .

Bar his number from your phone

Regretfully, if he withholds his number when dialling he will sneak through your security. You can bar his email address from your inbox too. Obviously, if he rumbles you and sets up multiple yahoo identities at stalker.com, it's sadly back to the drawing board again.

Don't be nice

For these guys, a smile means you're madly in love; even speaking to them gives them hope and a suggestion of a long-term commitment. Zoë's ex refused to believe it was over and would turn up unannounced and uninvited time and time again. At first she would try to talk things through with him, but that just encouraged him further. In the end, being blunt was the only solution. If he refused to leave, she would walk out. If he knocked on her door, she kept it shut, locked and bolted. If he phoned her up, he would just get the dialling tone.

Invent a boyfriend

And the sooner you can do it, the better. If he keeps calling
you even after you've made it clear you're off the market,
have a final stand-off with your stalker that sets out once and
for all that not only are you not interested, you are now also
not available. For polished duplicity, persuade one of your
male friends to pose as the amorously-inclined amigo.
Preferably, said friend should have more muscles than the
stockroom of a specialist seafood supplier, as well as a black
belt in an obscure martial art that enables him to immobilize
an opponent using just the tip of his little finger. Such skills
could come in handy one day (and it's a great party trick if
not). Hopefully seeing you in the arms of another will
galvanize your stalker into seeking someone else.

Change your phone number

Desperate times call for desperate measures. This was the last
resort for Hannah, who became the object of obsession for a
crazed Frenchman. Luckily he showed his bunny-boiler
tendencies early on in the liaison (the day after they met he
bombarded her with calls and texts to an astonishing degree
– alarm bells were ringing so loudly they'd have given Big
Ben a run for his money), so he didn't know her address.
This proved a godsend. In short, the Frenchman was
unhinged and wouldn't take no for an answer. Hanging up
didn't work. Barring his number had no effect. By the time
the heavy breathing started, he was no longer a nuisance, he
was downright scary – Freddy Krueger had nothing on him.

It was time for Hannah to change her number; luckily, Lionel didn't track her down (and frankly, dating a guy with a name like that, she was asking for trouble from the start).

• •

Sometimes, too, the men are not crazy, they're just not right. Here's our step-by-step guide to finishing with them kindly but firmly.

Let him down gently

The fact is his pride and heart are on the line. Judge how best to break up with him – people may despise or dismiss the email or text-message route, but if that's how you've generally been communicating (a likely scenario in this day and age), both styles have something to be said for them. Neither would put him on the spot for an immediate response, as telling him by telephone or face-to-face would do. And, let's be honest, it's a hell of a lot easier for you.

Let him take 'No' for an answer

You will find that some men can be quite taken aback to be knocked back. They simply can't believe it. They're astonished, confused, stunned –

you're breaking up with *them*? – so you may occasionally have to be blunt. Steven, having taken Kate out the month before and had subsequent date offers refused each week since, was still disbelieving when she finally emailed to say she didn't want to see him again ... ever. He emailed back to ask 'Why?' Kate then delivered the pièce de résistance – 'I don't think the chemistry's there, and as I'm looking for a *serious relationship* I don't see much point in dating again.' As predicted, the term 'serious relationship' soon cooled his ardour. Funny that.

Don't be afraid of finishing with him

Whether you're worried about hurting him, frightened of being on your own or just feel awkward being the 'bad guy', breaking up is always hard to do. But it's worth remembering that while Mr Wrong is on the scene, Mr Right may just miss his cue to enter your life. Like Gwynnie in *Sliding Doors*, if you don't make certain difficult choices, other opportunities may not happen. The blonde bob is optional, but the moral of the story is clear. Make the choices. Maybe break his heart. But if you're better off without him, it's a bitter pill worth swallowing. No matter how nice the guy, or how 'half-right' he is, *never* settle. It's better to be single and happy than in a relationship and miserable. Make like a tree and leave.

Independent Women

As this book has probably shown you, the dating game is full of more ups and downs than the Himalayas. Finding a man is not necessarily your problem, it's finding one who fits the bill that causes sleepless nights. But, while you're still looking for Mr Right, why not indulge in a few sleepless nights of an entirely different variety? The single life gives the kind of freedom all smug couples would give their shared DVD collection for. So why not take advantage of that? Stay out all night long at a house party full of people you've never met before, develop that flirtation with the man in the newsagents, enjoy the fact that you don't have to shave your legs every single day (unless you want to). Susie, a sexy singleton, recently took the party train to Paris: an evening Eurostar service to the French city, dinner and cocktails in the gastronomic capital of the world (what could be more elegant?), then disco dancing in a club crawl (indulging in not a few foxy Frenchmen along the way), before catching the 7 a.m. service back to London. Sounds like fun? Then why not do it? After all, who is there to stop you?

While you're living the single life, live it up as an amatory legend. Who said being single had to be all Bridget Jones and bitterness? Instead, be brazen and beautiful. The key element to being an amatory legend is to enjoy enticing men: not necessarily for your sexual satisfaction, but more for your flirtatious fun. You *don't* have to sleep with the men who date you – even your kisses ought to be hard won – but rather just enjoy being a sexy lady out on the town. Just have a good time and remember that flirting doesn't have to lead to friskiness ... unless of course you want it to. Being an amatory legend means that all the men will want you but they can't all have you. Believe us, such circumstances regularly lead to exquisite tensions ... and not a few floral deliveries to the office. What have you got to lose?

Your Guide To The Ultimate Flirtatious Life

No man is under your radar

From your colleagues at work to the man on the train who gives up his seat for you, every gentleman deserves a little saucy smile. They may not be God's gift to women, but you can guarantee that your benevolence will brighten up their day. Don't be a tease; be genuine in your affection. *You* know you're just saying 'Thanks for letting me sit down' – he's suddenly believing in the Lynx effect.

Being sexy is a state of mind

Even the most stunning women have their 'off days' – days when you feel as though Arnold Schwarzenegger is more feminine than you, and your hair has randomly decided that the bird's nest is *so* the 'in' look this season. We all have a fat day or a bad-hair day from time to time (and occasionally, if you are really unlucky, you experience both at once). On days like these, sometimes it really is best to go back to bed and wallow in gloom. On others, the right shade of lipgloss or the right pair of jeans can turn it around for you. Put a swing in your walk as you stride down the street, add a funky hat or headscarf to your outfit ensemble, and you're suddenly more Sienna Miller than Sienna Miller herself. And that's even without Jude as an accessory.

Any man you choose to flirt with is likely to reciprocate

This applies especially if you're currently 'on fire'. Every girl experiences these times – when all you have to do is step outside your flat to find men falling at your feet. Builders wolf-whistle at you, cars beep, and you're surrounded by studs 24/7. Frankly, if this is happening to you (and we're assuming you're not Cameron Diaz at this moment), take full advantage. Milk it for all it's worth. Smile coquettishly and live it up – feel like a million dollars, and if your admirers fancy spending the same on you, well, who are you to deny them? Accept all dinner dates, enjoy every dance, flirt your heart out and savour all the attention coming your way. Darling, you deserve it.

ℒ Don't be afraid of making the first move

Though some of you will be old-fashioned girls who couldn't imagine anything more embarrassing, in the modern dating world ladies can and do ask for dates. Why shouldn't we? After all, in the workplace we're now more confident in asking for promotions – and the same applies to romance. If you're not happy with your lot, then upgrade. You may be the only person who can make that happen. Face it, if you ask a guy out the worst he can say is 'no', and as far as we know no one's died from that yet. You'll also be safe in the knowledge that he will simply be kicking himself for ever more that he was crazy enough to turn you down. On the other hand, if you don't ask him out, you may never know what might have been – and an amatory legend should have no regrets.

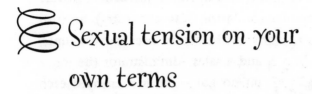 Sexual tension on your own terms

Basically, you can take your flirtations as far as you want. Don't feel pressured into anything. If the guy's got more animal magnetism than the combined residents of London Zoo, and all you want to do is rip his clothes off, then go for it. We've all been there, and is there really any need to resist temptation?

Alternatively, take the route of Laura, a confident lady with more than the occasional one-night stand on her sexual CV, who decided out of the blue one day that she was 'off sex'. Not off men, not off dates, not off the odd bit of tonsil tennis – but just off intercourse until she met someone really special. She stuck to her resolution, and not only found herself inundated with interest from the opposite sex, but also discovered that she felt sexier without the act itself. For Laura, knowing that she wasn't going to sleep with men gave her back some confidence that she felt she had been lacking. She was now back in control because she had set herself limits, and also felt that she had more respect for herself because of her decision. She went on to have a wild autumn featuring a gardener (lovely muscles), an actor (sexy chemistry), an Irish barman (the accent does it every time), and a sales administrator (he was a bit no go) – she just enjoyed each date, encounter, fling and fumble as they came and went. She wasn't looking for anything serious and felt she applied her sexuality to match. This life choice won't work for everyone, of course (and we should mention that she's now back on the rumpy pumpy, albeit with her long-term boyfriend), but it is important to remember to keep your sexual tensions *on your own terms*. That way no one gets hurt – you especially.

Be upfront about your intentions

On a serious note, remember that with your new seductive powers come new responsibilities. 'Being a bastard' works both ways. If he's falling for you and you just don't feel the same, then *tell him*. It may be he'll be happy to play it your way, but men – like women – sometimes want all or nothing, and if you don't feel that way inclined towards him, it's time to walk away, no matter how much fun you might be having. The guilt of humping and dumping him is a real rain on your parade, so ensure that you make the break cleanly and kindly. You've been on the receiving end when a man has messed you around and left you broken-hearted – so be careful not to treat them in the same scandalous way. Respect your man and make sure that you are both singing from the same song sheet – even if you do end up going solo.

✆ Accept all invites

You will only ever have this kind of independence and freedom once in your life – though of course that's not to say that you *won't* still be wowing them at tea dances in your eighties – so really make the most of it. Live it up. Turn your life into Party Central and you really will be having such a great time that finding a man who is right for you will be an unexpected bonus when it happens. Become an amatory legend and you may well find yourself part of a legendary love affair to end all love affairs … not to mention one that really is going to last.

• •

So there you have it. Think about that break-up back in the first chapter – haven't we all moved on? It's barely worth a first thought now, let alone a second. But humour us: look back on it for a moment and see how far we've come. The tubs of ice cream, the cigarettes and alcohol are things of the past (though always an optional extravagance). The comfort foods are simply not necessary now, when you're so comfortable in your own skin. Instead, your life is a whirl of opportunity and possibility, of parties and pulling prowess:

Don Juan has nothing on you. You are on fire, and nobody's going to put out your flames – so burn baby burn baby burn.

We hope we've honed your radar skills to an expert level. Though the occasional Mr Sub-Standard might sneak through when your defences are down, at least now you'll know what to do if he becomes your stalker. Those oddballs and mummy's boys won't get a look-in, and as for the players, they might as well go and play with themselves: you've had enough of their games. We can't promise you'll never get dumped again (some things come with no guarantee), but try to look at each split as a strength-builder, and remember he obviously wasn't right for you. Mr Right is still out there somewhere, and as we all know, when it works, it really works – so it really is worth waiting for.

In the meantime, don't let the dust settle on your party shoes. Holding out for The One doesn't mean putting a hold on your life. Indeed, it's often when you're not actively looking for love that Cupid comes calling. The ultimate flirtatious life is about having fun, with or without a special man in your life – and frankly, even if you are attached, there's no reason for you to lose your mojo. After all, that's why he fell in love with you in the first place. Be confident, big up your self-esteem and remember what you're worth: simply the best. Never settle.

So, you've been f****d. You've been chucked. And now you've bounced back. Think heels, frocks and fabulousness. Think cocktails and champagne. Think of the life you really

really want to lead. There may well be a few more frogs to kiss before you end up with your prince, but let yourself enjoy all the amphibian action along the way. What are you waiting for? Get out there!